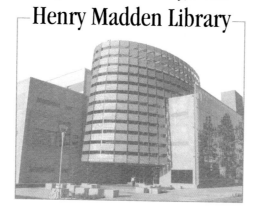

THE FINAL YEARS

New York, Ontario & Western Ry

by John Krause & Ed Crist

photos by Robert F. Collins and others

ISBN 911868-32-2

Library of Congress No. 77-77441

**To our children
Carolyn Lee Krause, and
Jennifer, Matthew, and Rebecca Crist**

Carstens
PUBLICATIONS, INC.

Fredon-Springdale Road **Fredon. New Jersey**
Address all mail to:
P.O. Box 700, Newton, New Jersey 07860

JOHN KRAUSE

TABLE OF CONTENTS

Acknowledgements

THE FINAL YEARS is possible only because of the help and assistance provided by many dedicated railroaders, railfans, historians, photographers, and others who unselfishly provided material, information, and time. The tremendous collection of Bob Collins opened up the entire prewar era, as did the collection of Fred Neusser whose NYO&W negatives are now maintained by the Ontario & Western Technical and Historical Society. Bill Wilcox provided a number of valuable photos and also aided in identification of many others. Ken Hojnacki provided access to the superb photos in the DeForest Diver collection housed at Cornell University. Ken was also extremely helpful in providing information on the previously unremarked Northern Division of the NYO&W.

O&WTHS associates Bob Mohowski and Marty Feldner provided the society and its magazine: a library of information which would have been unavailable elsewhere. Marty also provided working space, darkroom assistance, and encouragement and support. More photos came from Harry Zannie whose photos often had angles and scenes not otherwise recorded in the postwar era. Additional photos came from Rod Dirkes, George Krumm, Carl Munck, John Treen, Bob Haines, Jack Robinson, Walter Ruegger, Rusty Re-

cordon, J.D. Engman, Don Dover of Extra 2200 South, Bob Yanosey, Forrest Trittenbach, Marv Cohen, and Jeff Winslow.

Special thanks go to NYO&W veterans Guy Twaddell, the late Oscar Bennett, and Elwin Mumford for their first hand comments and assistance. Elwin went over the first draft with us and his clear recollection of places and events was reassuring to the authors. Mike Koch provided the cover painting by the late Manville B. Wakefield, one of the few Wakefield paintings not previously printed in full color. Our thanks also to Jay Diamond who graciously permitted us to borrow freely from his extensive collection of O&W timetables and other paper memorabilia. Additional help came from our friends at the Sidney Historical Association, the Chenango and Sullivan County Historical Societies, and the O&W Chapter of the National Railway Historical Society at Middletown, New York. Hal Carstens also provided the encouragement, technical assistance, and go-ahead which took the germ of an idea and turned it into the reality of print.

Perhaps, most of all, a thank you to Dorothy and Louise. Doing a book is akin to having a house guest move in with you and it requires a lot of tactical and moral support to carry it off. They both provided the help and encouragement needed, especially when a photo didn't print up quite right or a hot lead for information proved to be a false lead.

AN INTRODUCTION

Owen W.

My first look at the O&W came with a fan trip in June of 1948. My host was the New York Division of the Railroad Enthusiasts and our train was the regular passenger train with a new diesel up front and a special car on the rear for the fans. A far cry from the fan trips of the 1960's and 1970's, but in 1948 it seemed like Heaven to a fan just starting his photo collection. By July, just a month after this trip the O&W would kill the fire in its last steamer. Less than ten years later, the last diesel would tie up at Middletown for good. The O&W was quite literally a legend in her own time; she would be remembered as the railroad that should never have been built, and yet true or false, that would not keep her from earning a lasting place in the hearts of railfans.

I had the feeling that the time was right for a pictorial look at those final years on the O&W. Ed Crist and I had met at trackside in 1975 and learning of his interest in the O&W (he had just assumed the editorship of the O&W Technical and Historical Society's magazine), led me to believe that Ed would be the logical choice of a person to work with on this soft-cover book project. During the early months of 1976, Ed and I sought out collections that could turn up the photos we would need to illustrate the book. My own collection was limited; but with help, initially from Bob Collins and Hal Carstens and subsequently from many others, the necessary material was secured. Publisher Hal Carstens was immediately receptive to the idea since he too had always had a fondness for the road. Working with Hal again also brought back pleasant memories of railfanning together thirty years ago on the O&W and other roads.

After much planning and many trips and phone calls between Monroe and Rockville Centre, our book was well underway. I did the long hours of darkroom work and Ed poured out the words on the typewriter and steadily the layout began to fall together. Ed was able to provide the artwork and maps to go with the photos and text and together we wrapped it up to go to press.

Only the twilight years are shown in this book; the last years not only of steam but of the diesels that could not save the line. One of the first Class One roads in America to go diesel, she expired before a road switcher ever came on the property. Come take a trip with us back in time. Ed and I both hope that you will will enjoy our look at the O&W in *The Final Years*.

John Krause

Rockville Centre, New York
September, 1976

Twenty years have passed since that dreary March 29, 1957 when the New York, Ontario & Western turned its last wheel. Twenty years later we find a whole new generation of railfans and modelers having an intense interest in a hard-luck pike abandoned before many of these fans were born. It would be convenient to write it off to the current wave of nostalgia, and call the O&W a fad. There may be some truth in that. Perhaps in an age of Amtrak and Conrail, it may be simply more gratifying to retreat to what is supposed to have been a happier, simpler time.

For many of us, the O&W is a memory of younger days: an old friend who has passed on. Of course the older fans can remember the best days: the days of steam, passenger trains, long rumbling freights, all the trappings of a big-time operation. For those of us who are younger the memory is different: the last summers of passenger service, perhaps a treasured ride in a coach or up in the cab, the weeds that always seemed on the verge of swallowing up the rusted rails, and finally those impersonal seizure notices tacked up on the stations that spelled out the end of the line. For those of us who remember the O&W, the source of interest is obvious.

What about the legion of fans who never saw the railroad in operation or even its present day remnants? The railroads of Colorado, both narrow gauge and standard, invite a comparison for both have developed a host of admirers from afar. The interest seems to lie in the uniqueness. There was nothing like it in terms of equipment, operations, or any other criteria. There is also the element of the little guy. The O&W and the narrow gauge lines of Colorado were the antithesis of four track main line, hundreds of locomotives in a single class, and the whole concept of "systems." Both had their share of boom times and prosperity. Both had the right combination to stir the fan who looks beyond his own backyard.

In presenting this volume, we had a number of specific ideas in mind. First and foremost we make no pretense that this is a history of the O&W. There are others more qualified to write a definitive history of the railroad. What we have aimed for is a pictorial overview that will convey the feeling for the road: that imprecise amalgam of cars and locomotives and people and events that take a dollars and cents, nuts and bolts enterprise and turns it into a living and breathing entity all its own.

Because many of our readers are unfamiliar with the railroad, we have used a line of route approach, presenting the photographs in roughly station by station order so that the uninitiated can follow us on our journey over the Old and Weary. Finally, we have restricted ourselves roughly to the 1937-1957 time slot, corresponding to the development of railfan interest in the O&W: The Final Years.

To those of you who know the Old Woman, here is an opportunity to renew the acquaintance. For those of you who are meeting her for the first time, we are quite pleased to introduce you.

Edward J. Crist

Monroe, New York
September, 1976

A BRIEF HISTORICAL SKETCH

The O&W was born in the post-Civil War period; a time when the nation looked to territorial and industrial expansion to heal the wounds of internal warfare and reunification. The building of the transcontinental railroad perhaps best exemplified the sense of "manifest destiny" and inspired a host of less ambitious projects. Literally every village of any consequence felt that its future lay in a connection to the outside world over a road of iron rails on hand-hewn ties.

In October of 1865, a group of worthies gathered at Delhi in upstate New York to discuss the possibility of constructing a railroad from Oswego on Lake Ontario to the ports of New York. The principals were the Hon. Dewitt C. Littlejohn, former mayor of Oswego and then Speaker of the State Assembly, and Henry Low of Middletown, then a State Senator. There was much talk of an "air line" route until the more pragmatic matter of financing the new road came up. With the self-serving finesse that has made politician a dirty word, Littlejohn and Low rammed through a piece of legislation known as the Town Bonding Act, which allowed municipalities in the state to bond themselves for the construction of a railroad. This otherwise obscure piece of legislation would have a lasting effect on the newly formed New York & Oswego Midland, for their route wandered all over the state in an attempt to touch down on those communities which put up the proper amount of hard cash. Some hard-pressed New York taxpayers would have been quite indignant had they known that as late as 1970, they were still paying off some of these old Midland bonds. Unfortunately many of these villages would never fulfill the grand dreams they envisioned and the larger cities which already had

rail service would not commit tax dollars for still another line.

It took three years to hash out the meandering route and raise the money and the first spade of dirt was turned at Norwich in June, 1868. The construction proceeded with great difficulty, both in the field of engineering and finance. In typical nineteenth century fashion, however, the principals always collected a handsome salary no matter how anemic the treasury might be. After five years of ups and downs, the railroad was completed on July 9, 1873 and the next day saw the first through train from Oswego to Jersey City. The Midland itself terminated at Middletown, but had made arrangements to reach Jersey City via the New Jersey Midland. Initially the Oswego Midland had tied its fortunes to the New Jersey company, but later hard times would see the two go their separate ways. The New Jersey portion would become the New York, Susquehanna & Western while the segment from the state line to Middletown would eventually become the 14.5-mile Middletown & Unionville short line.

With typical Midland luck, the road was completed just in time for the Panic of 1873 and went into receivership the same month it was completed. The Receivers valiantly attempted to operate the line despite seizures of engines and rolling stock by irate tax collectors. After two years of incredible hardships their luck began to take an upward turn. The milk business which had begun as a single car in 1871 had grown to substantial proportions and the Centennial Exposition of 1876 added revenue dollars to the passenger accounts as New Yorkers flocked to Philadelphia to celebrate the nation's hundredth birthday. The road was up for sale and the black ink on the ledger books would not be ignored for long. It quickly attracted the attention of Conrad N. Jordan of New York, a banker representing some parties with an unusual interest in the Midland.

On November 14, 1879, Jordan bought the railroad for $4.6 million, a bargain basement price for a property that had cost a good $26 million to build. It seems in retrospect that his interest in the property was minimal and he was really acting as an agent for George Pullman and a number of associates who all shared a common dislike for Commodore Vanderbilt and his New York Central and Hudson River Railroad. Pull-

man had never forgiven Vanderbilt for using the sleeping cars of his arch-rival Wagner, and this was the chance to get even. He sent his vice-president Horace Porter off to New York to handle the project and his first task was to organize the New York West Shore & Buffalo. On January 21, 1880 the old Midland was resurrected as the New York Ontario & Western Railway and with the West Shore, jointly organized the North River Construction Company. The construction company was supposed to build the West Shore, utilizing some pieces of existing trackage and additionally build a branch for the O&W from Middletown to the Hudson River at Cornwall. It is futile to attempt to sort out the financial high-jinks of the three companies in the period from 1880 to 1885. The West Shore was built in fairly short order and the Ontario got their branch along with trackage rights to Weehawken and terminal facilities opposite New York. In the typical fashion of the period, the rich got richer (through stock manipulations) and the poor (the small shareholders) got measurably poorer, for the new West Shore got into a rate war with the New York Central. The well-established Central was more able to sustain this sort of blood-letting and eventually bought out the debilitated West Shore, strangely giving the O&W a very generous terminal and trackage rights agreement.

With the Pullman people gone and a new host of British and Dutch investors in their place, the Ontario proceeded to stake out its new place in the sun under the leadership of Thomas P. Fowler. The new president had come from a family with numerous railroad and steamship interests and the law school honors graduate had broken into the business as counsel to Vander-

CARL P. MUNCK

A.V. NEUSSER PHOTO: O&WTHS COLLECTION

bilt. If any single man can be credited with making something of the O&W, then it was certainly Fowler. He took the company from a run down ne'er-do-well and turned it into a first class carrier in all respects. His first year in office (1886) saw the lease of the Rome and Utica branches, originally short lines that had fallen under D&H control. His pet project, however, was the 54 mile Scranton division from Cadosia to Scranton which opened in 1890. Fowler knew that access to the coal fields of the Lackawanna valley would usher in a new era of prosperity and his forecast was correct. The new coal traffic put heavy demands on the railroad and Fowler poured huge amounts of capital into the plant, rebuilding and expanding facilities all along the line. At the same time the milk business and the passenger trade continued to grow; the O&W knew what salesmanship was all about and never missed an opportunity to promote any service that would add a dime to the bottom line.

By 1900 the O&W had acquired a substantial reputation among the New York area roads and that year they acquired the old Port Jervis Monticello & New York. Two years later the original line from Summitville to Ellenville was extended through to Kingston, giving the O&W the map it would retain until 1957. In 1904 the New Haven bought a controlling interest in the O&W for the apparent purpose of gaining leverage in their dealings with other roads. They could always threaten to use the Ontario to break out of their New England enclave. In the fall of 1912, President Fowler resigned and turned over the reins to his former vice-president John B. Kerr. The following year proved to be the peak for both passengers and milk and the O&W began, imperceptably at first, to decline towards insolvency.

The USRA operation during World War I left the O&W in poor shape and it took some time before the road began to enjoy the prosperity of a booming economy. Despite the good times, changes were being wrought. Improved state roads brought increased automobile ownership that was taking the customers out of the coaches in increasing numbers. The service cutbacks began in 1929 and by the early 1930's many parts of the road were freight only. The opening of new coal breakers in the Scranton area lifted coal tonnages to an all time high in 1932 and despite the depression, the O&W succeeded in paying dividends until 1935. The bottom dropped out rapidly as the mines began to play out after two generations of mining, and as strikes became more frequent. Gas and oil began to displace anthracite for home heating and coal tonnages fell rapidly. The final blow came in the spring of 1937 as two of the three company owned collieries failed. President Joseph H. Nuelle, who had succeeded Kerr in 1930, resigned and moved on to the D&H. The failure of the collieries caused the parent O&W to default on its bonds, and in lieu of a new president the O&W instead got themselves a court appointed trustee. On May 19, 1937 they filed Section 77 bankruptcy proceedings.

The job of saving the ailing road fell to Frederick E. Lyford, an experienced railroader who went to work trying to find new sources of income to replace the fading coal revenues. He attempted innovation in the passenger department and strived hard to capture for the O&W a share of the bridge traffic moving from the west to New England and Canada. The onset of World War II increased carloadings and perhaps served to mask the futility of Lyford's prodigious efforts. He resigned in 1944 and turned over the trustee's position to his former assistant Raymond L. Gebhardt and a new co-trustee, Ferdinand J. Sieghardt.

The team of Sieghardt and Gebhardt decided that salvation lay in a policy of dieselization and they pursued it until the last steamer was banished from the property in 1948. Passenger service was cut back progressively until September of 1953 saw the O&W join that growing number of roads in the Official Guide that carried the designation "Freight Service Only." The O&W's fortunes progressed from bad to worse in what has become a very familiar scenario, but which we must remember was unique at the time for a 500 mile Class 1 road. Labor relations degenerated after a 1947 strike with the O&W men working for substantially less than the national wage in an attempt to save their jobs. Shippers became increasingly dissatisfied with the serv-

ice and many connecting roads would not route a car O&W unless the bill was prepaid, assuring them of their share of the rate. Trustee Gebhardt died in 1953 and his partner resigned the following year, with the court naming a new Trustee, Lewis D. Freeman.

The legal hassles were becoming increasingly complicated and merely served to stymie the effort of local shippers, officials and unions to mount a grass roots campaign to save the railroad. Suggestions were made for sale to assorted interests and for breaking up the railroad into several short lines, but to no avail. Finally the Federal government intervened when railroad retirement taxes were not paid and encouraged the court to liquidate the property. Last-ditch attempts to save the O&W were fruitless and on March 29, 1957, lineside observers turned out to watch the last sad train head for Middletown, dragging a motley collection of equipment bound for sale or scrapping. Through the spring and summer of 1957, the equipment was sold off or cut up and small pieces of track were farmed out to other roads for operation. In August, scrap trains began the sad task of pulling up the rails.

And so it was over. For some the shock was great that such a large railroad could simply be abandoned and torn up, yet most of these people would live to see the debacle of Penn Central and the disappearance of six other venerable names into the colossus called Conrail. In a way and despite its uniqueness, perhaps the O&W was a harbinger of things to come. Too many of us chose to dwell on that uniqueness rather than on the similarities it shared with so many of its Northeastern kin. For now, let us ignore the legal entanglements, the rancor and difficulties and enjoy instead the engines, the trains, all the facets of the best of the O&W in The Final Years. ⊆

The locomotives of any given railroad are always one of its most prominent aspects. The family look of the motive power usually catches the eye at a very early stage. Put Santa Fe and Southern Pacific out in the same stretch of desert and there is no question of which was which. Similarly, the trackside observer at Englewood, Illinois had no trouble distinguishing between Pennsylvania and New York Central. For this reason we begin our look at the Old Woman with a study of her motive power. Interest in the NYO&W began in the late 1930's: the days of the Engine Picture Kid and the three quarter, rods down portrait. We must remember that early railfan activity was heavily concentrated in the New York metropolitan area and while most railroads were well into heavy modern power and rolling stock, the O&W still operated antique camelbacks and wooden coaches. In an abrupt turnabout, the O&W continued its uniqueness by becoming one of the first major roads in the region to completely dieselize. The O&W's early covered wagons would be it: the railroad would not survive long enough for the road to worry about acquisition of second generation hood units. So come along while our little friend Owen W introduces us to the cast of head end performers.

The Y class 4-8-2 built by Schenectady in 1922-1923, engines 401-410, were among the NYO&W's best looking locomotives and are occasionally referred to as USRA copies. Actually, Motive Power Supt. Burton P. Flory had his drawings and specifications laid out before the O&W Board of Directors, before the USRA design committee had finalized their plans for light Mountains. The chronic postwar shortage of cash prevented the company from purchasing the locomotives until more than two years later.

The light 400 proved to be Burton Flory's last complete design. When the O&W went shopping for new power in 1929, they took delivery on ten heavy Mountains which were near duplicates of the New York Central's L-2 Mohawks, although Flory details gave the engines an O&W look. The Alco construction numbers are spliced right in the middle of the numbers for the L-2 class. O&W nos. 451-460, Schenectady, 1929.

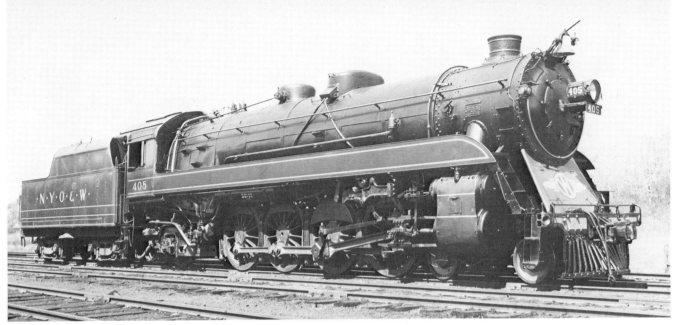

Owen W.

In 1937, fresh into bankruptcy, the O&W retained noted industrial designer Otto Kuhler to streamstyle their crack but dowdy looking Mountaineer on a slim budget. Kuhler worked a miracle with the sleek new train created from 14-year-old cars and power, and the results made headlines. The 405 is shown in her new garb at Summitville in the spring of 1940.

ROBERT F. COLLINS

The economies of the war years caught up with the Mountaineer and the 405 was quietly relieved of her superfluous sheet metal, retaining only the chromed handrails and stack bands that marked her former glory. In a game of musical chairs, the original tender had been replaced with a larger tender from a scrapped class X 2-10-2 while her original tender went to a needy class W 2-8-0. Taken at Middletown, August 24, 1946.

ROBERT F. COLLINS

9

Beauty and the beast. Above, the Flory designed Teakettles, built by Brooks in 1911, nos. 225-228. Only four engines but fast, graceful, and loved by their crews. If the class E Ten-Wheelers were praised, the class X Bullmooses, delivered the same year as Teddy Roosevelt's ill fated third party candidacy, were damned by every crew which ran them. The 2-10-2 types were built by Schenectady in 1915, engines 351-362. They were widely acclaimed in the trade papers when first built for their tremendous size and power. Alas, the size also wreaked havoc with O&W track and cost a fortune to maintain. A steady stream of Alco engineers visited Middletown through the 1920's in a futile attempt to make something of the class. Their efforts were in vain and the series were relegated to Scranton Division pusher service. An outmoded dinosaur of the drag freight era, they began going off to the scrappers as early as 1940, leaving behind sisters ten years older but eminently more serviceable.

Engine 304 at Middletown in the summer of 1937. The class W Consolidations were the O&W's all-purpose engines, showing up on yard jobs, mine runs, through freight and on passenger trains. The 26 engines, nos. 301-326, were built at Alco's Cooke Works in Paterson, N.J., in 1910-1911, and were equipped with signal lines except for 313 and 318 and steam lines, excepting 313, 318, and 325. Another of Burton Flory's designs, their arrival on the property was an unusual sight to the crews more accustomed to camelbacks. Their long high boiler uncluttered by a center cab prompted their nickname of Long Johns. The 304 retains her original tank on a replacement cast steel tender frame and was the only class W engine to boast a cross compound air pump.

Sister engine 311 under the Norwich coal dock in July 1948 was a class W-2 2-8-0. The W-2 was a result of a Federal regulation that locomotives exceeding 90 tons driver weight be equipped with stokers. The fireman's union persisted and the bankrupt company in a monumental bit of nonsense, retorted by taking ten of the class (302-308, 310, 311, 315) and adjusting the spring equalization and moving the air pumps up on the front deck to transfer an incredible 10.5 tons of weight to the pony truck. Apparently an equitable agreement was then reached for no more engines were rebuilt and stokers were never applied. Engine 311 is shown equipped with one of the original Bull-moose tenders displaced when the class X locos were given new larger tenders in the 1920s.

ROD DIRKES

JOHN KRAUSE

U-1 class 4-6-0 no. 244 poses under the coal pocket at Middletown in the summer of 1937. The class U locomotives were originally built by Cooke between 1901 and 1905 except for eng. 249 built by Dickson in 1901. Between 1916 and 1924, the Middletown Shops converted nine engines (241, 244-246, 249-251, 253, 256) from the original 2-6-0 wheel arrangement to 4-6-0's. All but one of the original Moguls were gone by 1940 but the Ten-Wheelers lasted right through the end of steam. The grand staircase of the U class from ground level to the running board was an O&W trademark later applied to many V and W class engines. A few classs U and V engines retained their original two bar crossheads but most were replaced with conventional alligator types when piston valves and Baker gear were applied.

Class V is represented by the 282 at Summitville on May 12, 1940. The 282 is listed on some rosters as having been scrapped in January 1940. Look closely at the cab number and you'll read 278 under the new white paint but 278 remained on the roster until 1946! The photo shows the original two bar crosshead, new staircase and pilot steps plus new cylinders and Baker valve gear. The original tank has a cast steel frame applied in the 1920's. Many afficienados considered the class V as having exceptionally fine lines as originally built.

The squat chunky class P no. 216 at Mayfield in July 1940 was one of twenty in her class, built by Cooke between 1900 and 1904. They were billed as the heaviest locomotives in the world when built, a title which quickly passed on to heavier power. The original high mounted acetylene headlight, wood pilot, D valves, Stephenson gear and a smaller tank riding on Fox trucks were all replaced as the years went by with more modern gear. Class P locos called the Scranton Division home since their heavy tractive effort, exceeded only by the Mountains and Bullmooses, made them ideal for service on the heavier grades of the Scranton line. The class survived almost intact up to the end of steam, and were often referred to as "Orries," a name reportedly acquired because of their similarity to the amply proportioned proprietress of a Mayfield watering spot frequented by O&W crews.

Engine 701, shown at Mayfield in May 1948, was the last steam locomotive bought by the O&W to help solve a sudden spurt of business in 1947, and was acquired from the D&H, their class E-3a no. 805 built by Dickson in 1903. 701 saw service on the O&W for less than a year and was sold for scrap in June 1948. Engine crews did not lament the loss, especially in view of the previous scrapping or sale of 13 more modern Mountain type engines. Photos of the 701 are relatively scarce.

Another product from the fertile mind of Burton Flory: the class L 0-6-0 switchers, nos. 50-56, built by Cooke and Brooks, 1910-1911. These were unique in being the only later day O&W power to have high mounted headlights rather than the standard O&W centered headlight. Class L lost its slide valves and Stephenson gear when superheating was introduced but retained their original tenders. The NYO&W cooperated with the Pilliod Company in the early development of the Baker valve gear which became standard for O&W power by the 1920's. No. 53 was snapped in May 1938.

Class I locomotives were actually two groups, the first lot, 30-39 being built by Cooke in 1903-1904, and the subsequent order coming from stranger Baldwin in 1907, engines 40-44. Like class U, the class I locos were delivered as 2-6-0's and in the 1919-1921 period, six engines (30-35) were rebuilt as class I-1 4-6-0 type. As with the U class, the unrebuilt 2-6-0 types did not fare well and all of the unrebuilt engines were scrapped in 1937 except for engine 42. 42 survived on the O&W roster until 1945 when it was traded to the Unadilla Valley in exchange for a worn out class V Mogul the UV had previously purchased. The UV bought themselves a diesel shortly thereafter and old 42 saw only limited service but did hang on until April 1956, very nearly outliving the O&W itself and becoming the last survivor of the O&W's steam fleet.

ROD DIRKES

MARVIN H. COHEN COLLECTION

In late 1941 and early 1942, the O&W took delivery of five new 44 ton diesel-electric locomotives from Alco-GE. The 44 ton weight was no accident since existing labor contracts called for a fireman on locomotives exceeding 45 tons driver weight. The maroon locos sported silver lettering and black edged silver striping, and were primarily assigned to Sidney, Oneida, Fulton, and Oswego. Unfortunately for steam, they made an impressive record. The O&W units were among the earliest units sold and O&W's experience with the mighty midgets was ballyhooed in Alco-GE promotional literature as an example of the economies of diesel operation. Nos. 101-105 retained their original paint throughout the war years. 102 is shown, above, in her original dress during a snow storm. As new EMD power arrived, management must have decided that the old Mountaineer colors looked out of place and the five pioneer units were repainted in the new grey and orange scheme. Following delivery of the 21 NW2 switchers from EMD in 1948, the 44 tonners were sold off to a variety of short lines. After 35 years of service, four of the five are still in operation. The little engines that could, survived not only the O&W but even the later fleet of FT and F3 road power. Below: 101 in the new scheme at Middletown on May 27, 1950.

Trustees Sieghardt and Gebhard realized in 1944 that the O&W's salvation would lie in dieselization. To pay for the new power they went to the depression-born Reconstruction Finance Corporation and secured underwriting for a loan of approximately $2 million. The order was placed with Electro-Motive in the fall of 1944, during the war years when only EMD was in a position to accept road diesel orders. In June 1945, the nine new drawbar coupled FT AB units were delivered by the Erie at Middletown, numbers 801-808. The ninth set was numbered 601 and was largely paid for by Standard Oil who used it as a testing laboratory. This left the 500 and 700 series vacant, possibly for additions of steam power numbers. Above, 802 leads a northbound freight out of the High Lights Yard at Middletown. The new units coexisted with the aging steamers until January 1948 when the first of three F3A units arrived, with two more following in February and March, units 501-503. These three units were intended for passenger service and were delivered with train lines. Not long after, the Middletown Shops applied footboards and still later the distinctive nose handholds. Steam heat boilers were passed up in favor of homemade heater cars since at this time only Trains 1 and 2 operated all year round. Below, left: 502 is seen at Cadosia in September 1948. In March 1948 the final blow to steam came with the arrival of four additional F3 AB combinations: numbers 821-822. Below, right; 822AB is shown at Maybrook Yard growling contentedly while Maybrook was invaded by a Lackawanna Rail Camera Safari on Oct. 17, 1948.

Dieselization was completed in 1948 with delivery of 21 NW2 switchers from EMD; 111-116 arriving in March and 117-131 coming in June and July. Unlike the first FT which was brought into Middletown for inspection by the brass and other appropriate publicity, the switchers were delivered at Sidney and placed in immediate service. Left, the brand new 112 works the Cadosia Yard. The classification lamps were salvaged from steamers. The switchman's garb is still from an age of steam.

In 1925 the O&W tried a cost cutting experiment on the Norwich-Oswego run. The brand new Sykes railbus no. 801, shown below, left, at Middletown, was an ugly duckling with no hopes of ever becoming a swan except for the number which later was transferred to an FT. The crews gave the units a choice assortment of names and the public was not impressed with the Spartan accommodations. The ridership continued to decline and the service was dropped in 1929. The 801 ended up in storage at Middletown where it was dismantled in 1939 with the body going to Roscoe for use as a storage shed where it still served as late as 1951. Other railcars, nos. 802-804, were all larger Brill products varying in details and all much better than the earlier Sykes unit. Even so, they could not stop the declining passenger revenues and were sold to the New Haven in the early 1930's. The 804, last gas-electric bought and the last sold, poses at Kingston in 1932.

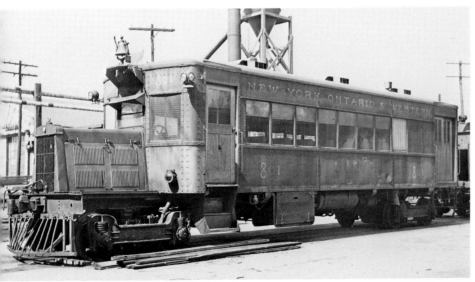

TWO PHOTOS BY 35 SLIDES, COURTESY ROBERT MOHOWSKI

 # WEEHAWKEN

Most of the railroads serving New York City tied up on the west bank of the Hudson River in New Jersey, necessitating a ferry ride to Manhattan. The joint West Shore-NYO&W facility at Weehawken was almost directly opposite the 42nd Street midtown area and travelers on the Old & Weary began their journey by ferry. The Weehawken terminal lay beneath the bluffs of the world famed Palisades and was reached by a 4225 ft. tunnel pierced through solid rock. The station tracks and ferry slips were south of the tunnel while the freight yards and towering wooden coal docks were to the north. By the late 1930's, the coal business had disappeared and only a single daily freight worked its way to Weehawken. Passenger business held out longer than the coal traffic. Holiday weekends in the late 1930's and early 1940's would see seven or eight sections of some trains roll into Weehawken to disgorge their flood of tired but happy vacationers into waiting ferry boats. On this page we see 227 wearing the green as she rolls into Weehawken soon to swing to the left onto the station tracks that lay perpendicular to the waterfront. The O&W was unique in that they would issue special timetables for holiday service, not only the national holidays but also for the Jewish and Christian religious holidays.

18

One prized specimen issued in 1932 is a joint Easter-Passover table. The Catskills, then as now, were famed for their resort hotels catering to New York's Jewish populace with religious services featuring opera stars turned cantor, mountains of delicacies appealing to Jewish tastes from both eastern and western Europe, and entertainers of movies and radio. Many well known stars broke into the entertainment field in these great old hostelries. Yarmulkas were a common sight on the male passengers riding the O&W. Below, the engineer of another class E 4-6-0, eng. 226, waits for the highball to roll north out of Weehawken. Just ahead of the engine can be seen the tunnel portal, while to the right of the interlocking tower are the leads to the freight yards and coal docks. Sandwiched between the fortress-like walls of the Palisades and the broad expanses of the Hudson River, the Weehawken Terminal was a mecca for train watchers and trolley fans who could see a variety of steam power of both the Ontario & Western and the New York Central, plus the big yellow trolleys of Public Service's Union City line.

The Y-2 class Mountains could rarely be spared from the Coxton-Maybrook symbol freights but Christmas Day 1940 found the 453 on the point of northbound Train No. 1, The Ontario Express, at North Bergen. Before tying up at Walton, the butterfly plow on the pilot of 453 might be put to hard use. Snow in the Catskills came early and heavy. Note the Scullin disc driver on the main axle, an O&W addition applied in the early 1930's. Middletown also added the forward sand dome to the Y-2's. Other than these details, there was little to be added to an exceptionally fine design.

C. GEORGE KRUMM

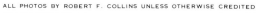

Engine 408 dusts the signal bridge at Little Ferry with cinders as she streaks south with a passenger extra past the strings of coal in the Susquehanna's yard.

The appeal of the high stepping class E 4-6-0's is obvious as the 227 crosses over at speed to the inside track for the non-stop run to Weehawken with southbound Train No. 8, The Roscoe Express, at Little Ferry in June 1940. The 227 sports a new stack, shorter and wider than the original. The addition made the engine steam more freely, but a careless engineer could easily pull holes in the best laid fire.

U-1 class camelback 245, built by Cooke in 1904, was rebuilt as a 4-6-0 in 1924. This June 1940 action shot shows her rolling through Little Ferry with a southbound extra. The closed windows and vintage equipment suggest an empty run to Weehawken to pick up vacationers heading for the Catskills for the July 4th week as the summer season blossomed into peak traffic.

Just 22 months and a whole world of difference. Above, northbound Train No. 1 at West Englewood behind engine 402 in July 1946. Her Franklin trailer truck booster made her the sole occupant of the Y-1 class. Below, May 1948 and we're several hundred feet from the first location and it's still Train No. 1 but the sharp staccato bark of 402 has been replaced by the whining grumble of 501. The 402 is still alive and on July 21st she'll roll into Norwich with a northbound freight, drop her fire, and write the final paragraph on steam on the O&W as the last operating steam locomotive.

A northbound O&W freight gathers speed after climbing the Teaneck hill into West Englewood in February 1947 with 807AB easily handling a load of empty hoppers out of Weehawken. The water column would see service for another five years by New York Central steam and was used by O&W steam only in cases of emergency.

JOHN KRAUSE

HAROLD H. CARSTENS

West Englewood again on a near perfect spring day in 1948 with F3 501 easily handling the nine car southbound train. The end of the 1948 season saw the passenger service cut back from Walton to Roscoe. Only one of the four tracks is still in service as this book is written. When operating on the West Shore, O&W trains carried New York Central train numbers and were listed in the West Shore timetable.

DU

From a perch inside DU Tower, photographer Harry Zannie record-ed the northbound Roscoe Express (above). Dumont was the end of four-track and a commuter train storage yard, and the tower con-trolled the funneling of trains onto the double iron. The RPO and observation car running backwards have been repainted to match the diesel color scheme.

Engine 805 with a northbound camp special composed entirely of New York Central coaches passes Dumont Tower on the express track, June 30, 1947. Since no stops were to be made, the NYO&W special is using the express track.

Above, Towerman's view from Dumont Tower with Jersey Central No. 876 2-8-2 easily handling the nine car all-coach train of leased equipment. Only a study of the timetable would tell you the train was O&W. Engine 876 arrived after the war and stayed for some time afterwards. Earlier visitors included DL&W 1200 and 2100 Mikados and New Haven 4-6-2's. Curiously, the New York Central which provided trackage rights and leased coaches did not provide motive power to the O&W. Other coaches were leased at various times from the Seaboard, Atlantic Coast Line, New Haven, Lackawanna, Reading, and Jersey Central. The heavy summer traffic made renting more economical for the O&W than investing in new equipment. Above, right; sister CNJ class M-63 Mikado 889 heading north through Dumont with the eight car Mountaineer, Train No. 3. Although the cabs were berated as being cold and drafty to work in, the Central Mikes made a good impression on the O&W enginemen. Following World War 2, freight service below Cornwall into Weehawken was largely restricted to a single freight daily in each direction. If the southbound freight made its run during the dark of night, the northbound run was available to the alert and patient photographer. Right, this Dumont scene of Esso's rolling laboratory, Eng. 601 with a string of empty hoppers, was taken June 30, 1947. 601 was equipped with a variety of monitors for use in testing various lubricants and fuel.

In 1947, the big building boom was barely starting and Haworth, 15 miles north of Weehawken, still retained a rural flavor. Railfans were accustomed to filming New York Central Pacifics, Hudsons, and Mohawks, and rarely an 0-6-0 or a Boston & Albany Berkshire. O&W's No. 1 was welcome relief, shown above headed by Eng. 402. Home rails were still 34 miles ahead, with four miles to the New York state line.

Below left, northbound Train No. 1 rolling through West Nyack, N.Y. five miles over the state line. West Shore tracks are drifting eastward back towards the Hudson and nine miles ahead 822 will plunge into the 1620 ft. Haverstraw Tunnel and emerge near the west bank of the historic Hudson Valley.

Below right, West Point Station as seen from the cab window. The station was always immaculately maintained and in 1955 played host to CNJ camelback 774 for the filming of "The Long Grey Line." West Shore engineers were forced to construct a tunnel exactly one half mile in length to pass the granite outcropping that forms the point.

CORNWALL

At Cornwall, 52.2 miles north of Weehawken, O&W trains would return to their home rails, after first stopping at the West Shore's Cornwall Station for passengers, shown at right. Below, the 882 eases gently over from the smooth, well-ballasted West Shore double tracked mainline to the more primitive, lighter railed O&W main, to pick up orders and clearance from the towerman at CN Tower. The tower, shown at the bottom, controlled not only the O&W main but also provided protection for O&W crews crossing the West Shore tracks to work the coal docks. Cornwall had once been the terminus for many of the coal trains originating on the Scranton Division, prior to the big slump in coal business in the early 1930's. The structure was neatly removed from the books on the night of September 18, 1952 when a burning Liberian freighter attempted to dock there in order to extinguish a deck fire. The ship fire was extinguished but the dock burned to the waterline in a spectacular inferno that could be seen three miles inland. Just past the Dock Road Crossing near the tower can be found a stone monument commemorating completion of the West Shore Railroad in 1883.

BOB YANOSEY COLLECTION

WILLIAM S. WILCOX

HARRY ZANNIE

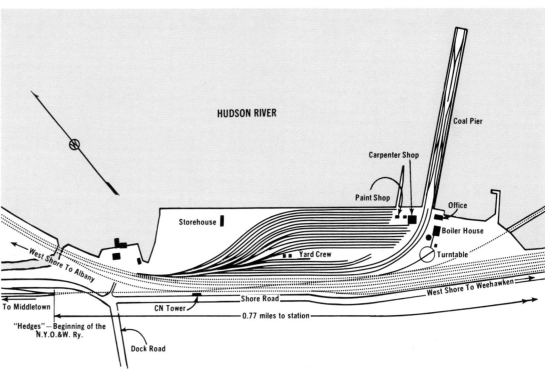

HUDSON RIVER

Coal Pier

Carpenter Shop

Paint Shop

Office

Storehouse

Boiler House

Yard Crew

Turntable

West Shore To Albany

West Shore To Weehawken

To Middletown

CN Tower

Shore Road

0.77 miles to station

"Hedges"—Beginning of the N.Y.O.&W. Ry.

Dock Road

27

ROBERT F. COLLINS

In a photo of near-classic proportions, Class E Ten-Wheeler 227 heads northbound Train 1 up the 1.50% grade nearing Firthcliffe. The tracks have left the river grade and are climbing towards Dennistons, the crest of the grade near Little Britain. When the coal business was booming, nearly all northbound freights, mostly empties, required a pusher out of Cornwall. Even in later years, a job known as the Cornwall protect engine was stationed there to assist northbound passenger trains. To the right, another classic in gingerbread: the Firthcliffe station. All the stations from Cornwall to Middletown had been built during the abortive West Shore venture, all two-story wood buildings with agent's living quarters upstairs. Firthcliffe's design was unique while the remainder were identical standard types. Firthcliffe remained open until the end and was handled by one of the only three women agents on the whole line. The stretch from Cornwall to Firthcliffe was used for a number of years after abandonment by the New York Central to serve the local Firth Carpet Company (from whence the station got its name). Eventually the service was discontinued, the track torn up, and the station became a victim of arson. The name Montana engraved in the end of the building was the original designation for the station, carried only a few years before the carpet company moved in.

D. DIVER COLLECTION, CORNELL U., COURTESY KENNETH L. HOJNACKI

The junction at Campbell Hall was one of the most important on the railroad, especially in later years, providing access to the bridge traffic from the New Haven at Maybrook that the ailing carrier needed to survive. The view at right was recorded by Hal Carstens in June 1946 from the rear of a northbound Railroad Enthusiasts excursion looking south towards Burnside. In the distance, the former double-track now trails into a single line. The removal of the second track also saw the closing of CH tower as CTC was installed from Campbell Hall north to East Branch (82 miles). The station bore no resemblance to others on the line for it had been built originally by the Central New England & Western around 1890, the year the CNE arrived at Campbell Hall via the massive Poughkeepsie bridge. The CNE was absorbed by the New Haven in 1904 and when New Haven passenger service was dropped in the late '20's, they sold the building to the O&W. Along with Firthcliffe, Campbell Hall survived until the end, the only two open stations south of Middletown. The track swinging left past the station is the old CNE lead into Maybrook. At the bottom, a northbound freight coming out of Maybrook is about to pull by CH station and pick up orders. Note the disparate combination of color-light signals and lower-quadrant semaphores. Crews were never tied up at Maybrook. They would either bring a train or come light from Middletown, pick up their train and work back through Middletown to tie up at the Lehigh Valley's Coxton Yard near Scranton.

HAROLD H. CARSTENS

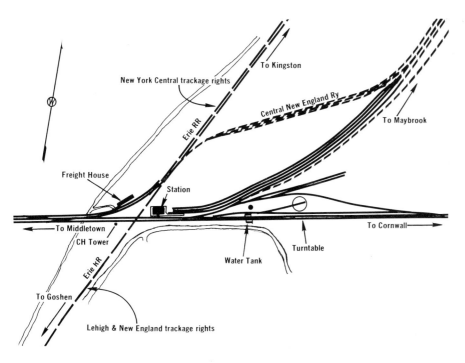

HARRY ZANNIE

29

Below, northbound Train 1 is braking to a stop at Campbell Hall. The high-boilered Ten-Wheeler and the wooden baggage car are more reminiscent of post-World War I than post-World War II and explain much of the O&W's charm; within 60 miles of New York was this veritable time machine that could take the fan back thirty years for the price of a coach ticket.

ROBERT F. COLLINS

Above, second LB-4 crosses over to the northbound main heading down to the station to run into Maybrook. The BL and LB trains were part of a through service via the New Haven, O&W, Lehigh Valley and Nickel Plate for Boston-Chicago routings. The BO and OB trains were mainly Lackawanna-O&W trains. Both routings were aimed at capturing some of the huge traffic flowing between the Buffalo and Maybrook gateways. Competing DL&W-L&HR and all-Erie routings made for fierce competition and the O&W needed every car they could get. The 459, a Y-2 Mountain, had 57 cars on her tail. In all likelihood, first LB-4 was filled out with the hot reefers and the second section took the leftovers. These trains carried so much fresh meat in refrigerator cars that they were often referred to by the crews as beefers.

HARRY ZANNIE

JOHN KRAUSE

If the ghost of the Old Woman is present at Campbell Hall, she must be shaking her head ruefully for she knows that only a few months remain before the fried egg herald on the tattered nose of FA 705 will join her own logo in that growing number of once-proud names and insignias that have disappeared from the Official Guide. The Lehigh & New England suffered the same fate as the O&W, but without the trauma of a twenty year bankruptcy. When revenues began to decline the parent Lehigh Coal & Navigation simply decided it was time to get out of the railroad business. Campbell Hall station survived until the early 1970's when the building, having become both an eyesore and a hazard, was mercifully destroyed by a controlled fire.

MAYBROOK

Left, No. 804 exchanges notes with New Haven FA's and GP7's at the Maybrook engine terminal. The all-covered-wagon roster is possibly one of the O&W's appeals to the younger fan. The once-maligned first-generation diesels have been rediscovered by a generation who grew up with them. Above, No. 822 shares the westbound departure yard with FA's of the Lehigh & New England. Note the early example of piggyback on the head end. The L&NE would survive the O&W by less than five years, ceasing operations on October 31, 1961. Below, 822 poses under the hump at Maybrook while waiting for its westbound run. The date is October 17, 1948 and the 822 seems well-recovered from her earlier traumatic experience when the brand-new 822 and sister 821 struck a rock on the tracks at Butternut Grove north of Cook's Falls. The boulder rode under the pilot of the 822 until it struck the north switch of the passing track, whereupon the four engines and seventeen cars piled up in all directions. The services of New Haven wreckers from Maybrook and the DL&W hook from Scranton were required to untangle the mess.

Bob Collins went out on a cold February 23, 1946 and recorded this improbable combination rolling out of Maybrook to Campbell Hall. Just outside of the yard, W-2 class Consolidation 311 is sending up a column of white smoke high into the crisp air as she gets a northbound extra under way to Middletown. Not so remarkable, you say—but wait, what's this on the rear? Teakettle 227 digs in to give the 311 a hand. The motive power people must have been really short that day. How many other roads would use a 1911 vintage light passenger engine as a helper? The grade from Campbell Hall to Middletown topped out at 1.2% right up through the city and to stall a train over any number of grade crossings was to incur the wrath of the city fathers. Of note also is the caboose cut in ahead of the helper. The O&W 8300 hacks (built at Middletown in 1916-18, 1924, and 1933-35) couldn't be trusted not to fold up and normally the pushers were cut in ahead of the hack, a time-consuming procedure. In the late 1930's the O&W was cutting up older engines with serviceable cast-steel tender frames. By taking two old frames and judiciously cutting and splicing them together by welding, they came up with a very substantial underframe that could be installed under existing cabooses and obviate the need for keeping the pushers ahead of the hack. At least one brand-new car, the 8360 was built on these frames and others were applied to older cars. We could never determine if the railroad ran out of old tender frames or money, but not all the cars were rebuilt.

Left, it's nearing summer's end as the stream-styled 405 leads a second section of southbound Train 8 (the Roscoe Express) over the Walkill River bridges approaching Campbell Hall from the north. Just ahead, the 405 will duck under the Erie's Graham Line for the last lap down to Campbell Hall station.

Below, No. 228 southbound with Train 8 below Stony Ford trailing a mixture of steel and wood equipment on a late August day in 1941. The E class Teakettles always seemed to show an exceptionally clear stack.

The last traces of snow have yet to disappear on this March day in 1942, but No. 459 has already shed her butterfly plow. The Y-2 Mountain is working hard on a northbound freight out of Maybrook as it rolls by Stony Ford with its cattle ramp. By the early 1940's the railroad was closing and demolishing most of the stations south of Middletown. Only Firthcliffe and Campbell Hall would survive until 1957. Today the only remaining station stands at Mechanicstown (1976), a private residence purchased from the railroad in the early 1940's.

ROBERT F. COLLINS

ROBERT F. COLLINS

No. 228 with northbound Train 7 heels into the bank of the curve approaching Middletown. The curve was very nearly a semicircle and skirted a ridge on the east side of town to bring the O&W into the city, side by side with the Erie and the Middletown & Unionville. The curve had an official name sanctioned by the Engineering Department, long since forgotten. Its more colorful name was inspired by a house of pleasure which stood for many years near the juncture with the M&U.

The hub of the O&W was the massive brick and sandstone station and offices at Middletown. Built in 1892, and designed by the noted station architect Bradford Lee Gilbert, who also did Chicago's Illinois Central Station and the rebuilt Grand Central Station, it replaced an earlier wooden structure. In 1936, the center section of two floors was added to accommodate the staff which had moved to Middletown from the expensive New York offices. The ground floor contained the famous Seeholzer's restaurant, where three generations of hungry passengers fed themselves in haste during the O&W's famous ten-minute meal stops. The company was apparently never convinced of the merits of dining cars and persisted in the archaic practice of meal stops right up until the end of passenger service. The station still stands (1976), the ground floor a nightclub disturbed by the occasional passing of a Conrail freight to Fair Oaks and Pine Bush. Originally the O&W leased the shortline Middletown & Crawford to get out of Middletown to the north. In return for a lease on the Erie-controlled line, the Erie itself was granted trackage rights to Crawford Junction where they went back on their own rails for the short hop to Pine Bush. When the O&W closed, the Erie resumed their own operation and added a short stretch of former O&W track to Fair Oaks. The line fared well through the subsequent EL merger, but faces an uncertain future under Conrail.

HAROLD H. CARSTENS

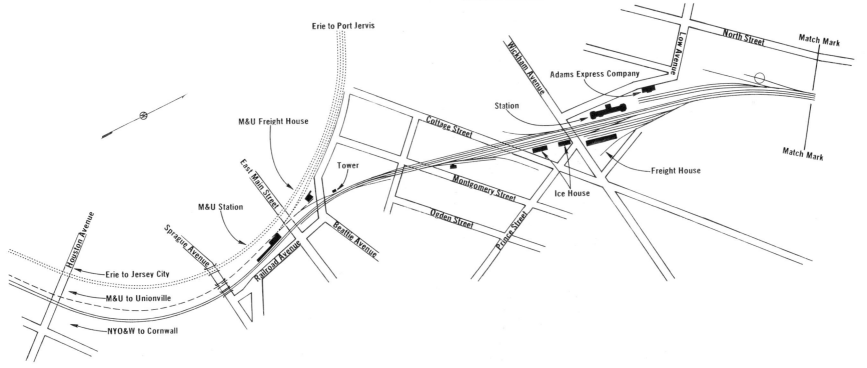

Southbound 4th No. 4 has departed Middletown station and is getting a roll on the train. Just ahead lies Washington Avenue crossing and the left-hand bank of the curve out of town. It's Labor Day weekend in 1940 and the hoards of vacationers bound home from the Catskills after the final summer weekend require the services of five and six sections of regular trains to get them all back to New York in time for work and school. The Memorial Day and Labor Day weekends, marking the beginning and end of the summer season respectively, brought out every available car and locomotive in an attempt to handle the sea of people bound to and from the mountains of Sullivan County. To the left lies the somewhat weed-obscured main line of the Middletown & Unionville and their primitive coal dock.

Two views show the area south of the station where the O&W and the M&U paralleled each other. On the opposite page, bottom, northbound Eng. 803 eases down the former northbound main approaching the East Main Street station of the M&U, a timetable stop for most O&W trains in former years. It's April, 1948, and the second track has been out for almost two years. The M&U was reorganized as the Middletown & New Jersey in 1946 and has retired its last steamer, an ex-O&W 4-4-0, in favor of a GE 44-tonner. In the opposite direction across the bridges, we see one of the 500 series F3's, right, leading southbound Train 2 past the M&U's rudimentary facilities. The now-useless turntable and water tank will soon disappear.

JOHN KRAUSE

A.V. NEUSSER PHOTO: O&WTHS COLLECTION

Northbound Train 3, the streamstyled Mountaineer, pauses at Middletown on September 4, 1939. This is the last weekend of summer service and 405 and her consist will go into hibernation until the following May. At least one other fan is out on the platform to record Otto Kuhler's handiwork. The streamstyling project was quite an innovation for the period and received plenty of ink in both the fan magazines and the trade press.

It's May 27, 1950 and although summer is just around the corner, there's still enough of a chill in the mountain air that the heater cars built at Middletown from old Y-class tenders are still being carried through to Roscoe. Walton service was cut off at the end of the 1948 summer season and Roscoe was the northernmost terminus for the remaining five years of passenger service. F3 units 821 A and B and heater car are exchanged for an identical set headed by the 822. Nearly all trains changed power at Middletown. The heater cars HT-1 and HT-2 shown here comprised the entire roster of the curious hybrids.

Southbound Train 8, headed by leased CNJ Mikado 876, waits patiently while the passengers gobble down a late breakfast at Middletown. Despite the meager ten minutes allowed for meal stops, you can be sure that the riders won't pass up Seeholzer's famous pastry before departing the Wickham Avenue station for the trip south. The date is July 5, 1947.

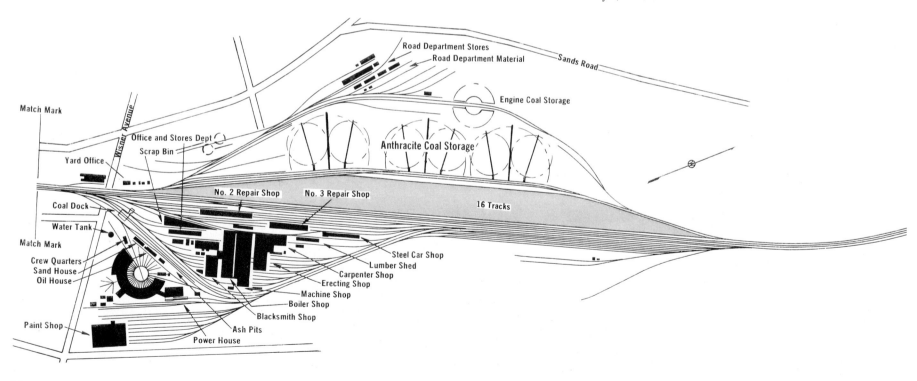

Eng. 121 lies on the roundhouse lead just a few blocks north of the station and just south of the Wisner Avenue crossing. Behind her a snowplow and flanger bask in the May sunshine, enjoying a well-earned rest. Across Wisner Ave. and directly above the cab of the 121 is the yard office. It's 1950 and the open area behind the yard office is void of the massive coal storage piles which once dominated the scene.

Just what did the streamstyled 405 do all winter before returning to the Mountaineer each Memorial Day? What else? She hauled freight and even did a few stints as a pusher out of Mayfield on the Scranton Division. A streamstyled pusher engine must surely be unique in the annals of railroading. A nasty-looking March 16th in 1941 finds the 405 heading north out of Middletown with BL-1 bound for Coxton. It's a pretty safe bet that the maroon "bib" of the 405 will be wearing snow before the junction at Cadosia is reached.

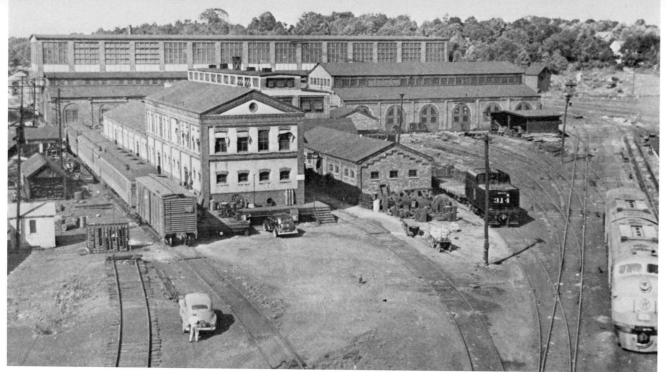

O&W engineer DeForest "Pat" Diver had spent a lifetime recording the railroad he worked for, and although he retired from the right-hand side in 1943, his interest in and his affection for the Old Woman continued unabated. Realizing that the new diesels would alter the face of the terminal he knew so well, the veteran engineman climbed to the top of the coal dock (shown in detail at center) to record these panoramic views of the Middletown terminal. Clockwise from lower left, the expanse of the North yard will remain mostly unchanged in future years, but the coal storage conveyors at left have outlived their usefulness and will

FOUR PHOTOS: D. DIVER COLLECTION, CORNELL U., COURTESY KENNETH L. HOJNACKI

soon come down. Coal storage facilities had been erected at Middletown and Cadosia at the turn-of-the-century to equalize the seasonal demand for coal. We are looking north and on the east side of the main stood the service facilities. In the background, a line of coaches wait their turn through the car shop. The large erecting shop complex was one of the best-equipped shops in the East and did a variety of contract work in later years as every source of income was exploited. Material was processed through the storehouse in the foreground. The sandhouse, ash pits, and powerhouse all lay next to the 26-stall roundhouse.

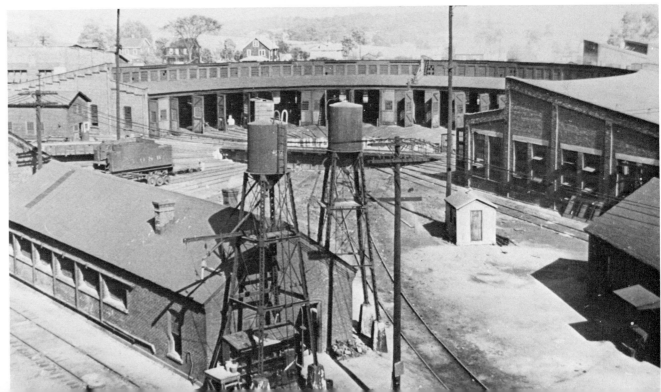

Eng. 227, laying down some good old-fashioned coal smoke heads northbound Train 7, the Roscoe Express, out of the north end of Middletown yards. Just ahead she'll cross over the Erie's Graham Line and head out for Crawford Junction.

Below, W-class 2-8-0 323 poses on the ash pit with the powerhouse showing in the background. The ash cars in the foreground were part of an original order for 1350 coal hoppers placed with American Car & Foundry in 1910-1911 to protect the bustling coal traffic. Virtually identical to D&H cars of the same period, they were relegated for the most part to Company service by 1940. The O&W's last new car order was for steel hoppers from Bethlehem Shipbuilding in 1929 and as a result, they suffered in later years with heavy-per-diem payments on foreign cars, for virtually none of their own equipment was fit for interchange service.

ROD DIRKES

ROBERT F. COLLINS

Eng. 324, heads a peddler freight north out of Middletown approaching Crawford Junction and the diverging Erie Line to Pine Bush. Strange looking milepost to right of photo was originally a Delaware & Hudson Canal mooring post. The O&W acquired a quantity when they purchased the canal right-of-way from Summitville to Kingston. A few still remain a monument to the builders of both the railroad and the canal.

Left, it's July 7, 1940 and southbound Train 4, the Mountaineer is headed by the 409. Is it a second section or is the streamstyled 405 in for shop work? In any case, she's out of the last curve and heading into the Fair Oaks speedway for the last leg into Middletown. Note the double headed semaphore signal almost up to the horizontal to mark the 409's passage. The main tracks were signalled from Cornwall to just above Cadosia and used a somewhat unusual two-headed lower quadrant system. The top head contained only two lights, red and green, corresponding to the two positions. Red was horizontal and green was downward at a 45° angle, with the top blade being pointed on the end. Similarly, the lower blade with its fish-tailed end gave indications of yellow and green. In service the stop indication was red-over-yellow, both blades horizontal. The caution indication was green-over yellow, the top blade down and the bottom blade horizontal. The clear indication was given by both blades pointing downward, giving a green-over-green indication; these were the only combinations used. The signals from Campbell Hall to East Branch were replaced by three-color block signals when CTC was installed, while the remainder of the old semaphore signals remained in service until the railroad closed.

43

Left, it's a balmy July 5th in the busy and power-short year of 1947, and leased New Haven L-1a class 2-10-2's 3210 and 3214 with some breathing space between them are working hard as they approach the Orange-Sullivan County line. The high-stepping is all behind them now and it's a lot of curves and hard pulling ahead to make the High View tunnel. The train is on the southbound main even though the train is headed north, since the northbound main has been removed from service and will soon be pulled up.

At the lower left, V-class Mogul 278 is drifting easy down the grade past Winterton depot, heading south towards Middletown. It's another golden summer day in 1937; one of photographer Bob Collins' earliest visits to the Old Woman and the beginning of a very rewarding friendship. Railfan interest apparently hasn't picked up yet, for the engineer seems quite amused that anyone would come out to trackside to record an antique center-cabber. In the next few years, he'll become quite accustomed to the curious visitors. Turning south, Bob didn't have much of a wait before sister engine 277 and U-1 class Ten-Wheeler 245 popped around the curve heading north with a camp train. Note that 278 carries the formal initials on her tender while 277 wears only the O&W herald on her tank. The O&W would not allow pushers to work through High View Tunnel so southbound trains out of Summitville would cut off the pusher on the north side of the tunnel. The pusher would wait for the train, while it traversed the tunnel and came down to Winterton to wait for the pusher to join them again. The move was time consuming but made necessary by the descending grade to the Shawangunk Kill bridge, where the pusher would be needed again back up the short but stiff grade to Fair Oaks.

THREE PHOTOS: ROBERT F. COLLINS

Left, the 803 is lashed up with the Esso test unit 601 as they dig in for the grade up to High View tunnel. They're past Winterton depot and climbing into the mountains of Sullivan County with a northbound extra, on March 24, 1946. Note the white flags on the 803, the O&W also used white sheet-metal "flags" to denote extras as long as the scheduled passenger service was run.

ROBERT F. COLLINS

D. DIVER COLLECTION. CORNELL U., COURTESY KENNETH L. HOJNACKI

Left, the High View (Bloomingburgh) depot, built in the late 1890's. Its stucco design would be copied by a host of the resort hotels during the 1920's. The economical stucco construction became so widespread and popular that it acquired the tag of Sullivan County Mission style, and abandoned examples of it still proliferate throughout the county. Just below the station stood BX tower which guarded northbound movements through the single-track High View tunnel. The tunnel, known variously as High View, Bloomingburgh, or Shawangunk, was one of the major headaches of the original Midland construction. Begun in November of 1868, the bore was not punched through until October 1871 and the first train finally passed through in January 1872. The mountain was a mass of loose shale and clay and the tunnel was a constant danger to crews. A masonry liner was installed in 1878 and again in 1897, but right up until the end, falling rock from the ceiling made train crews wary of the 3850-ft. bore. At right, a view from the cab of northbound Train 1 about to enter the longest tunnel on the line. The scaffold-like structure on the right was exactly that: a movable platform which could be run into the tunnel for maintainence crews to use in repairing the cantankerous ceiling.

HARRY ZANNIE

A.V. NEUSSER PHOTO: O&WTHS COLLECTION

Left, a southbound oil train behind Y-2 Mountain 458 passes the Mamakating depot. The north portal of the tunnel lies about a half-mile ahead. The 458 is probably being assisted by a pusher on the stiff climb out of Summitville up to the tunnel. The date is March, 1942, and German submarines have driven the oil out of coastal tankers and onto the rails. Oil trains required exceptionally careful handling since the sloshing of the oil magnified the slightest bit of slack action and a careless engineer would suddenly find himself with drawbars and knuckles spread all over. The Mamakating depot was sold by the railroad to the Veterans of Foreign Wars in the 1940's and still survived (1976) under the VFW's care.

Right, a cold December 1, 1940, and the 405 is cutting the crisp air with a sharp exhaust as she walks up the hill out of Summitville with a southbound Veteran's Special. In the valley below, the village of Wurtsboro once played host to the coal boats of the Delaware & Hudson Canal (the village was the namesake of the Wurts brothers, founders of the canal company), and still saw the passing of the Port Jervis and Monticello freights of the O&W. Employee specials were quite common on the O&W and persisted even into the early 1950's.

On the opposite page, photographer Nuesser recorded this unusual view of the north portal of High View tunnel from the rear of a northbound train. Steam and smoke continue to pour from the bore and over the years, the deadly concentrations of smoke and gas in the tunnel claimed the lives and limbs of many employees. WX tower to the right controlled the approach of southbound trains from Summitville and with companion BX tower on the south side, was abolished after the Second World War with the introduction of CTC.

The date is February 18, 1946, and the ground is surprisingly bare of snow as FT 805 gets southbound NE-6 moving out of Summitville. The dynamic brake housings are particularly evident in this photo. Not seen are the Middletown-designed hot air recovery units, an ingenious bit of engineering which took the heated radiator air and fed it back through a sheet metal housing to the engine intakes, thus sparing the 567 engines the shock of ingesting cold mountain air. In warm weather, the housing slid back on the roof out of the way to allow conventional aspiration. To the right, the Kingston branch local departs behind steam, carrying a baggage car just ahead of the hack. The track at the extreme left is the Port Jervis and Monticello branch line.

ROBERT F. COLLINS

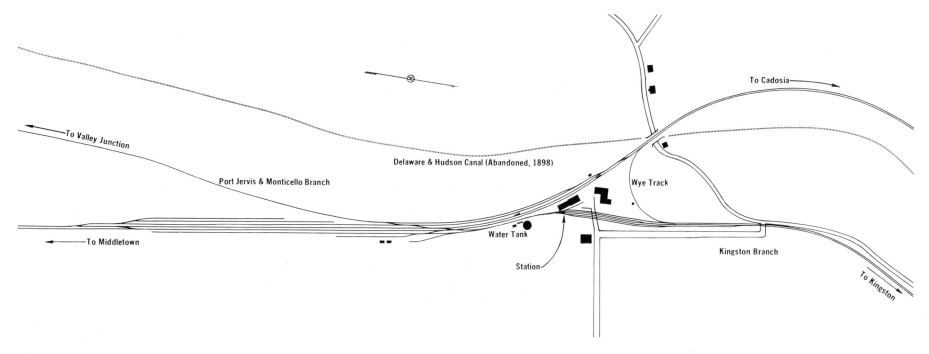

To Cadosia

To Valley Junction

Delaware & Hudson Canal (Abandoned, 1898)

Port Jervis & Monticello Branch

Wye Track

To Middletown

Water Tank

Station

Kingston Branch

To Kingston

Southbound 2nd LB-4 gets under way on a bleak March 16, 1941. The uncommon Elesco open feedwater heater below the cab is in operation and the swirl of steam around the tender from the stoker exhaust will soon be joined by the billowing exhaust clouds of the Franklin trailer truck booster. All Y-2's had trailer boosters. The Franklin booster had been initially tried out on Y class Mountain 402. An earlier experiment with a booster on a class X Bullmoose was deemed a failure. The extra 11,230 lbs. of tractive effort was really appreciated by the enginemen when trying to start a heavy train. Freshly-shopped engines would often be sent to break in as pushers at Summitville. Although the station still stands (1976), it's hard to imagine standing there today that the same spot once saw the ground-shaking passage of giants like the 456.

TWO PHOTOS: ROBERT F. COLLINS

Northbound BL-1 leaves Summitville behind the 404 for the assault on the 29 mile grade to Young's Gap. The name Summitville was deceiving, for the station lay in a valley with helper grades on both sides. The name was a remnant of the D&H Canal days when the area marked the top of the climb from the Delaware River at Port Jervis to the flat lock-free area from Summitville north. Note the mail crane to the right and the north leg of the wye off the Kingston branch just to the left of 404's pilot.

Northbound trains leaving Summitville faced the worst grade on the railroad: the 2% Red Hill grade. Over the years, the hill had extracted its toll in lives and equipment and enginemen descended it with great care. The scenery leaving the valley was unparalleled and the passenger traffic people in happier times strained the language considerably extolling the natural beauty of the highlands. In the view left, we see the short Little Falls trestle just south of Mountaindale and its namesake from the cab of a northbound diesel.

Below, photographer Collins, having caught a brace of 2-10-2's just below Winterton (p. 44), was sufficiently impressed to take advantage of the delay at Summitville to cut in a pusher, and use the extra time to get ahead of the train for a second shot nearing Woodridge. Engs. 3210 and 3214 are off the 2% Red Hill grade but are still climbing and the barely distinguishable plume of the pusher in the distance indicates that the battle against gravity is far from over. A good 17 miles remains yet before they top over the summit at Young's Gap. Note that the second track has already been taken up here.

In April 1942, the 227 with southbound Train 2 skirts Conklin (or Tierny's) Pond as it approaches Fallsburgh station from the north. The summer season has not yet begun and wartime gas rationing was about a year away. The abbreviated consist of Train 2 was more than adequate.

HARRY ZANNIE

A.V. NEUSSER PHOTO: O&WTHS COLLECTION

A fireman's-eye view of a meet at Fallsburgh (actually South Fallsburgh, but not on the O&W timetables): a southbound freight headed by FT 803 rolls by the depot, heading downgrade to Summitville. A few thousand feet ahead lies the 1023 ft. Fallsburgh tunnel. Like all O&W tunnels, it was never double-tracked and was protected by towers on both ends. When Monticello passenger service on the branch was dropped in 1930, Fallsburgh became the station where a connecting bus line took the traveler on the short hop to the county seat. The station still stands (1976), housing the local police and fire departments.

51

A.V. NEUSSER PHOTO: O&WTHS COLLECTION

The towering trestle across the Mongaup River was one of the many trestles and bridges that made the O&W such an expensive road to build. The area between the Neversink River trestle below Fallsburgh and the Ferndale trestle was a much easier stretch than either Red Hill or the 4 mile climb from Ferndale up to the Gap. The original iron bridge at Liberty Falls (the old name for Ferndale) was replaced in 1901 by a new steel bridge to accommodate the new and heavier power that the O&W was buying. To minimize delay to trains, the engineers constructed the new bridge 19 feet east of the old one, using the existing bridge as a construction platform. This was an engineering trick that the O&W had pioneered in 1894 during the rebuilding of the Lyon Brook bridge on the Northern Division. A year later, the Board of Directors voted to double track the road from Cornwall to Cadosia and in lieu of disturbing a year old bridge, the engineers simply went back and constructed a new bridge for the second track on the old piers, giving Ferndale its characteristic staggered bents. Ferndale was once the detraining point for the famous Grossinger's resort and the station remains (1976). Below left, northbound Train 9 (the milk train) crosses the structure behind the 409 in April 1943; while below, right; 1948 finds diesel power on the now single track bridge.

CARL P. MUNCK COLLECTION

HARRY ZANNIE

52

ROBERT F. COLLINS

The famous 405 rolls northbound Train 1 by the Liberty station on March 13, 1946. Liberty could probably be deemed the epicenter of the great Sullivan County resort industry. The O&W, beginning in June of 1880, issued a free promotional booklet entitled "Summer Homes" listing the accommodations available and generally promoting the hotels, the railroad, and the milk business. The issues of the early 1900's were very elaborate publications exceeding 150 pages, complete with original lithographs detailing the bucolic charms of the county. As the passenger trade declined with the resorts, the booklets became less and less ornate until they were finally dropped in 1950. From 1897 to 1904, the O&W also published a companion "Winter Homes," extolling not the scenic beauty but the healthful atmosphere of the mountains in an attempt to encourage what was then a growing business in tuberculosis sanitariums in the Liberty area. Friction arose between the two groups and in the long run, the hotel-keepers won out over the sanitariums and the O&W quietly dropped the publication, removing the ubiquitous physician "Dr. O. Zone" from the public eye. The mythical character appeared frequently in the editions of "Winter Homes" and in companion newspaper ads. The station at Liberty, like that at Middletown, had been designed by the architect Bradford Lee Gilbert who maintained a rural retreat further up the line. Built in 1893, it burned to the ground three years later, but was promptly replaced by an identical structure. It survives (1976) as a tavern, boasting an extensive collection of memorabilia of both the railroad and the resort industry.

Two days before Christmas of 1946, 806 approached Liberty from the north with a 40-car southbound extra. On an equally snow covered February 11, 1940, O&W engineer De Forest "Pat" Diver braved the cold to record these two views of the Liberty area. Below left, northbound Train 1 behind a U-1 Ten-wheeler crosses the Upper Liberty trestle, so-called to avoid confusion with the Ferndale trestle below Liberty. The cut at the south end of the bridge is the same one seen at the right past the 806 and was the first of many on the last torturous three and a half miles from Liberty to Young's Gap. The numerous cuts in the area of the Gap and the 1840 ft. elevation combined to make the area an annual winter headache for the railroad as the cuts packed tight with drifting and blowing snow. Below right, Pat Diver recorded three of his worthy brothers laboring together to lift a tonnage train up the hill. The 407 is assisted by a second engine ten cars back and a third pusher is just out of sight below the cut, about where we first saw the 806. The piers in the foreground once carried an exceptionally dangerous highway bridge which was eliminated by the state in the 1930's. The veteran engineer was shooting from the new Route 17 bridge and this type of state-funded road improvement was responsible for the continuing decline in passenger receipts.

ROBERT F. COLLINS

D. DIVER COLLECTION, CORNELL U., COURTESY KENNETH L. HOJNACKI

D. DIVER COLLECTION, CORNELL U., COURTESY KENNETH L. HOJNACKI

Livingston Manor was probably the busiest spot on the railroad that was not a major terminal or junction. It was the origin point for the wayfreights north to Cadosia and south to Middletown, and for the Saturday only Livingston Manor Limited, Train 53, and The Half Holiday, Train 27. Other summer trains originating from Roscoe would pick up their parlor cars at the Manor. The station, above left, like so many others on the Southern Division, replaced an earlier structure which had proved inadequate to handle the increasing business in the early years of this century. A restaurant was operated in the station, not for travelers so much as for the numerous employees who worked out of the Manor. All southbound freights picked up a pusher at Livingston Manor for the assault on the north side of Young's Gap. At 1.25%, the grade was somewhat easier than the south side, but still stiff enough that few trains could cross the divide unassisted. At the right, the famous 402 sits in the clear south of the station awaiting the next trip up the hill. Both coal and water were available here as well as a wye for turning engines. The 402 didn't rest very long; below, southbound LB-4 rolls into town behind Y-2 Mountain 457 throwing a monumental cloud of smoke and steam in the air to advertise her arrival. Let's wait just a minute; 457 has to have water and the fire probably needs cleaning, while sister 402 has to get out on the main and couple up to the train. Now turn the page and watch LB-4 get out of town. You can almost hear the deafening noise as the 402 digs in, determined to keep a good part of the slack bunched up tight.

THREE PHOTOS: ROBERT F. COLLINS

ROBERT F. COLLINS

HAROLD H. CARSTENS

To the right, southbound Train 2 lies in the clear at Roscoe awaiting departure time in August of 1951. After 1948, this was as far north as the passenger trains operated. In the distance lies the bridge over the Beaverkill. The O&W in its editions of "Summer Homes" made a special appeal to fishermen to come and try their luck on the Beaverkill and the Willowemoc. Indeed the predecessor Oswego Midland and the O&W had both seen fit to stock the streams with trout at their own expense to encourage the passenger business. The work was taken over in the 1890's by the State Fish Commission, which used a specially constructed coach to transport live fingerlings across the state for stocking trout streams. Roscoe station was even adorned with a trout weather vane. Four lanes of New York Route 17, the Quickway, occupy the area where Roscoe station and the 503 once stood.

Above left, in the summer of 1932, southbound train Train 4, the pre-Kuhler Mountaineer, leaves Roscoe, passing the wye on the left. The limited consist will be filled out with additional coaches and parlor cars at Livingston Manor while the crew registers the train. The O&W's fleet of parlor cars were almost entirely turn of the century vintage wooden cars and were named for the rivers and streams along the line. Above right, 16 years later, the 249 has been scrapped and the Mountaineer has been dropped from the tables. Southbound Train 2, the Ontario Express, is the sole remnant of the O&W's once-bustling summer passenger service. She's in the hole at Roscoe waiting for a northbound freight to pass before heading out. Train 2 with the 502 on the point has a carload of New York Division Railroad Enthusiasts on board. It's a 1948 RRE excursion. The fans dropped off at Cadosia for dinner at the famed Hancock House while the train continued to Walton, turned and headed back, pausing at Cadosia to pick up the well fed contingent of fans. This was photographer Krause's initial visit to the O&W and among the mementos of the day is the rare shot at right of the northbound 4 unit combo heading out of Roscoe. Supplementing the winking lights of the crossing flasher, a watchman with his hand held stop sign also guards pedestrians against the passage of the growlers.

The station at East Branch just after the scrapper's train had passed through in August of 1957. Note the piles of fresh cut lumber in the background, now relegated to truck transport. The entire area of Sullivan County was heavily forested and at various times supported sawmills, tie plants, tanneries, charcoal and acid factories; all carloadings to the O&W. Most of these industries fell victim to technological changes that rendered them obsolete, while the natural beauty of the area became more accessible by automobile with each passing year, thus dealing a double-barreled blow to the O&W's revenues. Down track to the left in earlier years was the connection with the Delaware & Northern. The D&N left the O&W and crossed the Beaverkill just above its confluence with the East Branch of the Delaware River, following the valley of the East Branch to a connection with the Ulster & Delaware at Arkville. The D&N was originally projected as a bridge route from Schenectady to Wilkes-Barre, but only this small 37.52 mile portion was ever built. It ceased operations in October 1941 and was sold to the City of New York. Today much of the former roadbed lies beneath the waters of the Pepacton Reservoir. The inset shows East Branch in happier times, as southbound Train 2 approaches from the north behind a class E Ten Wheeler. East Branch was one of the very few long tangents on the entire Southern Division and the time freights would roll through often at a mile a minute clip. The stretch from East Branch to Cadosia was the first on the road to be single-tracked in 1936. Today this is the main street of the tiny hamlet of East Branch and the station survives (1976) as a craft shop, while a portion of the right of way to the north has become a secondary county road.

GUY P. TWADDELL   INSET: JACK ROBINSON   JOHN KRAUSE

Right, the trees frame a mixed lash-up of F3's and FT's heading south along the East Branch of the Delaware with southbound NE-4. The Maybrook bound freight is south of Peakville (Trout Brook station on the railroad) and although we can't see it, time is growing short for the Old & Weary. The track followed the river from East Branch to Cadosia, where the waters of the East Branch terminated their northwesterly flow to join those of the West Branch flowing south towards the ocean.

Hawk Mountain was a jagged outcropping of granite populated chiefly by rattlesnakes. The East Branch of the Delaware made a very sharp bend around the mountain, but the builders of the Oswego Midland were forced to tunnel through. Constructed in 1870, the 1130 ft. tunnel was only slightly longer than Fallsburgh Tunnel but the hard rock made construction tough enough. Two towers, Hawk Mountain to the south and Wheeler on the north, protected the single-track tunnel. On the opposite page, we are looking down the length of southbound Train 12 shortly after popping out of the south portal of Hawk Mountain. A strange system: the Ontario Express ran as Trains 1 and 2 on the weekdays, but on Sunday it went north as Train 37 and came back as Train 12. The streamstyled 405 is in charge of the train on this February Sunday in 1940, while the inset shows sister 404 bursting from the north portal later that same year. Photographer Nuesser unintentionally captured an unusual effect: the head end is mirrored in the window of parlor car 83, the "Orange."

58

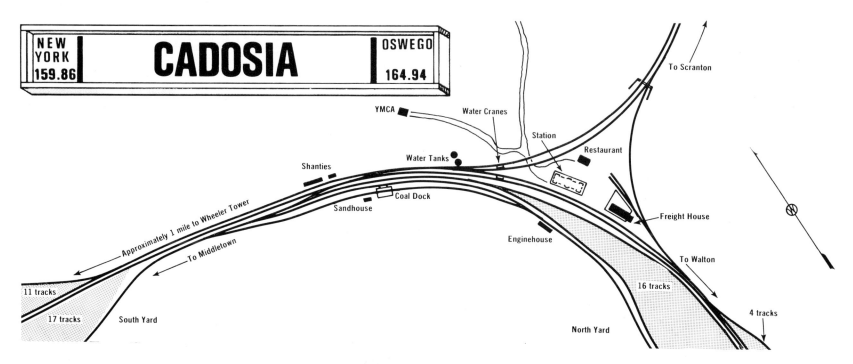

YMCA

Water Cranes

Station

Restaurant

Water Tanks

Shanties

Water Tanks

Coal Dock

Sandhouse

Freight House

Approximately 1 mile to Wheeler Tower

To Middletown

Enginehouse

To Walton

To Scranton

11 tracks

17 tracks   South Yard

16 tracks

North Yard

4 tracks

JOHN KRAUSE

Cadosia was the vital junction point of the Scranton Division with the main line, and in later years when the Maybrook-Coxton symbol freights became the lifeblood of the ailing road, this was as far north as many of the trains operated. The year is 1948 and northbound 805 is strung out through the South Yard as the FT-set prepares to cross over to the Scranton Division main, roll past the station and out on to the Cadosia trestle for the run to Coxton. The South Yard has had much of its trackage removed by this date and the coal storage piles near the tunnel have been done away with; victims of the decline in coal traffic. Note the ominous acetylene and oxygen tanks lying near the coal dock, a relic no longer needed.

A cold Sunday in February of 1940 finds the 405 heading up Train 37 as it rolls through the South Yard. At the south end of the yard lay Wheeler tower, guarding the north portal of Hawk Mountain tunnel, and the coal storage piles similar to those at Middletown. Today the entire area is occupied by the four lane concrete of the Route 17 "Quickway" and the Hawk Mountain tunnel is obliterated by a massive cut through the mountain.

HAROLD H. CARSTENS

ROBERT F. COLLINS

July 6, 1951 finds NW2 122 sunning herself in front of Cadosia station. The three year old switcher has the company of a veteran caboose: old-timer 8011, constructed at Middletown in 1883. The 8000 class was followed by a large group of four wheel bobbers in the 8100-8200 series before the O&W decided that eight wheels had been the right idea in the first place. Rebuilt at Middletown in 1905, the 8011 and two equally ancient brothers survived until 1957. Note the sliding-sash windows and the recycled passenger car trucks.

Opposite top, the 502 backs down on her train at Cadosia in June 1948. The F3 is preparing to depart north to Walton in what will prove to be the last summer of Walton passenger service before the cutback to Roscoe.

On the opposite page, two views of southbound Train 2 at Cadosia in the final days of passenger service. Left, former parlor car 83, the "Orange," converted to a coach in 1943, is more than ample to handle the dwindling number of fares. The local postman is busy loading mail sacks from his vintage pickup. To the right are the freight house and a portion of the station behind it. On the head end (right), the crew has time to chat before departure. Note that the 502 has yet to do away with the tradition of denim overalls and jumpers. The milk cars on the head end from the Breakstone dairy at Walton are not O&W. By 1948 most of the O&W's vintage wooden milk cars had been retired.

The 803 (above) has crossed over to the Scranton main and the fireman is out in the doorway to pick up the orders for the run to Mayfield. The 803 will remain a northbound train despite the fact that the Scranton Division runs roughly southwest. The anomaly was introduced in the late 1920's when the Coxton-Maybrook through freight service was inaugurated and the time-table direction of the Division was changed. This was done to avoid a direction change at Cadosia. At the same time the Southern and Scranton Division crews began running through without change from Maybrook to Coxton, one of the very earliest instances of interdivisional pools. The time is June, 1948 and like the coal dock, the water tanks and columns are living on borrowed time. Our photographer is standing under the eaves of Cadosia station looking south.

Owen W.

ROBERT F. COLLINS

ROBERT F. COLLINS

JOHN KRAUSE

JOHN KRAUSE

We close our section on Cadosia with a selection of views of the most well-known visitors at the junction. Opposite top, class W Consol 310 in front of the single stall enginehouse, Cadosia's sole facility for housing locomotives. Note the unusual location of the power reverse. Opposite bottom, class Y Mountain 408 still sports her original tender but has acquired a new mechanical lubricator, the only noticeable change made since her delivery in 1923. Above, FT-set 805 on the ready track. Note the sheet-metal extra flags just under the side window. The number on the nose just below the headlight was added by Middletown shortly after delivery and the rather dark gray of the bodies faded in later years to an almost pale blue, although the engines remained in tip top mechanical condition right up until the last days. Right, the 114 has just arrived from Sidney after delivery from EMD by the D&H as witnessed by the stack covers still in place. However, the boys have been busy: the pair of salvaged class lights are in place, and they've hung a push pole and rerailers on the flanks. Most likely they're waiting for some brass from Middletown to show up before cranking up the NW2 and pushing the 2-8-0's further north to their final holdout at Norwich.

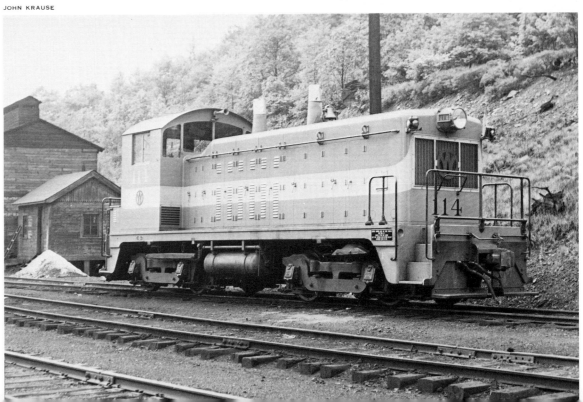

ROBERT F. COLLINS

Southbound Train 50 leaves Apex bound for Cadosia. As wartime gas rationing took effect, the bus companies became more and more hard pressed to provide service. Eventually the Office of Defense Transportation ordered the O&W to provide additional service and they added three Norwich-Cadosia trains: 50, 52, and 54 south, and 51, 53, and 55 north. Of particular concern to the government was the Scintilla aircraft magneto plant at Sidney and the trains were timed largely to accommodate the shift changes at the defense plant, with a generous layover allowed. The automatic block signals ended near Apex and further north protection was provided by operators using a manual block system.

WALTER J. RUEGGER

With the end of the war the only train left above Cadosia is the hardy 1 and 2. From the observation platform of Train 1, photographer Ruegger records the descent of the 502 down the 1.41% grade approaching Rock Rift. The verdant fields in the valley will soon be submerged under the waters of the Cannonsville Reservoir. Another of the many reservoir projects of the City of New York, this one employed the West Branch of the Delaware.

NEW YORK 179.43 | WALTON | OSWEGO 145.37

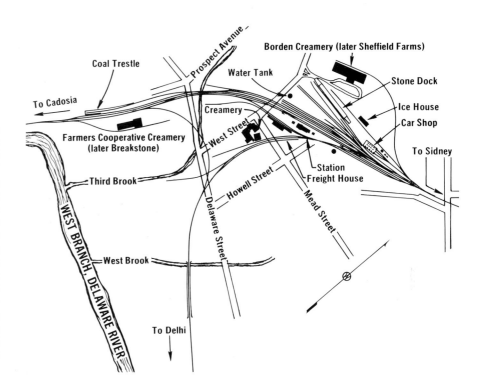

Walton, like so many of the O&W terminals, lies in a valley with stiff grades on both sides. To the south, the climb was 1.41% to Apex, while the northbound climb to Northfield tunnel was just a hair steeper at 1.42%. Walton was an important manufacturing town and dairy center. The 16.84 mile branch to Delhi began here and as late as the early 1930's, was served by the "Delhi Flyer," Brill gas-electric car 804 which connected Delhi with Utica; probably one of the very few trains to originate on a branch, run on the main, and terminate on a second branch. Mixed train service to Delhi, even more incredibly, managed to survive until 1947. In the summer season, Walton would be the northern terminus of Trains 1 and 2, the Ontario Express. Originally running the full length of the line, they were cut back in 1933 to Walton for the summer season and Roscoe in the winter. The few passengers going further north were accommodated by a rider coach on milk trains. By 1948, the summer business wasn't sufficient to justify the run and 1 and 2 were cut back to Roscoe to run out their last five years. Below, we see Walton in good times and bad; at the left, northbound Train 39, the Walton-Sidney peddler gets under way as the head man climbs on. Many of the head-end cars came from the Borden's creamery complex in the background behind the engine. The two head cars and a number of others are Middletown-built milk cars, although the O&W had other series of both milk and refrigerator cars and would even press plain box cars into service during the peak years of the milk business. At the right, the substantial Walton station sits in the summer sun of 1957, awaiting the arrival of the scrappers. Today the area is largely occupied by a supermarket.

CARL P. MUNCK COLLECTION

WILLIAM S. WILCOX

67

Left, the 405 stands at Walton awaiting the southbound return trip of Train 2 as the visiting firemen and spouses inspect the area. The occasion was a 1946 RRE excursion on 1 and 2.

Below, it's W-2 class 2-8-0 311 drilling a Breakstone's milk car on the north leg of the wye. We don't know if they're just working the yard or if they're putting together the mixed for the run to the county seat at Delhi; another important source of milk revenues, even in the declining years of service.

Below, the south portal of Northfield tunnel. Leaving Walton, it marked the summit on the northbound trip to Sidney. The second largest tunnel on the line at 1639 feet, it was opened in 1890 to replace the old Zig-Zag, the torturous set of switchbacks that had been originally employed to cross the mountain. Water freezing in the tunnel had been such a problem that a boiler house was constructed on the north side near Merrickville station to furnish steam to the tunnel for keeping the bore clear of ice. Near the Merrickville station stands (1976) the only surviving water tank on the line.

Descending from Northfield Mountain, the old Midland engineers encountered a small valley near Sidney Center, known as Maywood on the railroad. To maintain a usable gradient, they were forced to span the hill and valley combination with a pair of trestles known as bridges 216 and 217. Originally all bridges were assigned a number, counting from Cornwall. As some were filled and new ones constructed the system became useless and was replaced with a milepost designation. Above, a northbound fan trip on August 18, 1940 is strung out on the longer bridge 216. Above, right; the train is over the short hill between the trestles and photographer Nuesser is out on the side again to record the smaller bridge 217, as the pair of Ten-Wheelers, class E 228 and class U-1 245 approach Maywood with an eight car consist bound for Sidney. The cows on the hill and the creamery directly behind the station set the stage for the photo at the lower right. The 305, a W class 2-8-0, is heading southbound milk train Train 10 up the 1.25% grade out of Sidney heading for Maywood where a stop at the creamery is surely on tap. The 305's train includes a Sheffield Farms milk car, an O&W reefer and Borden tank containers fastened on flat cars, an interesting ancestor of today's container trains. Bringing up the rear is the accommodation coach for those few passengers riding south; all-in-all, a vignette of simpler times that have disappeared forever.

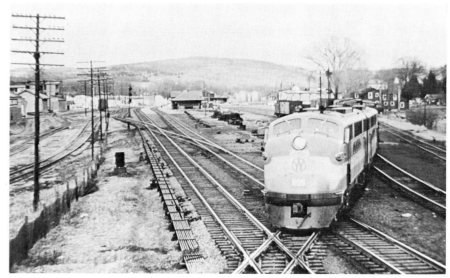

Sidney, not quite midway between Weehawken and Oswego, was chosen as the division point between the Northern and Southern Divisions. Around the turn of the century there was a great deal of local agitation to move the shops there from Norwich, but to no avail. In earlier years many trains originated and terminated at Sidney, but as the number of Northern Division trains steadily declined, the terminal became less and less busy. At Sidney, the O&W crossed the D&H (the old Albany & Susquehanna line), and the tower protecting the diamond was the only one besides Cornwall still open when the railroad closed. At the right, we're up in the tower watching FT 805 cross the D&H, heading north to Norwich just a few days before the road finally quit on March 29, 1957. In the background can be seen the Union Station of the O&W and D&H. The station and freight house were a joint venture of the two roads and were opened in the spring of 1913. The map below shows the location of the original Sidney station, and the new structure was approximately 150 feet north of the crossing. Today the entire area is occupied by a shopping center, the D&H is single track and the station is gone, although the freight house still sees service (1976).

35 SLIDES, COURTESY RICHARD L. RECORDON

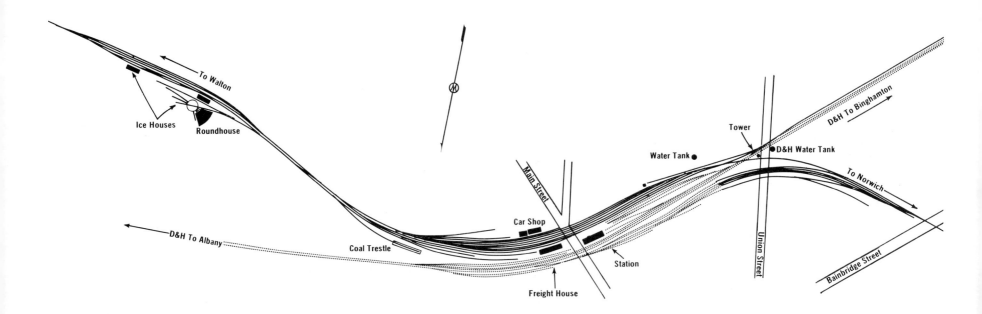

In 1948, that final year of steam on the O&W, railfan Krause was without an automobile to track down the elusive steamers, but fortunately, there was enough passenger service available to get an eager fan to where the smoke and steam was. Coming out of New York on the Erie to Binghamton, an Albany bound D&H train delivered our man to Sidney and a date with L class 0-6-0 53, shown right, resting near the car repair track just south of the Main Street crossing. It was a study in counterpoint as the 1911 camelback, the last of the class, dozed quietly on the sidetrack, its slumber disturbed occasionally by the thunderous passage of a modern D&H Challenger on the nearby main.

At left, it's September, 1939 and the southbound milk train has a contingent of upstate fans along for the ride. I-1 class 4-6-0 35 is laying in the clear on the yard tracks behind the station with a W class 2-8-0 heading up a local freight. The fans are inspecting everything in sight and chatting with the engineer. The milk will be turned over to Southern Division Train 12 for the trip to Weehawken, while the fans turn around and head back for Oneida as northbound Train 9. Like 1 and 2 on the Southern Division, 9 and 10 were frequently filled with fans in the late 1930's and early 1940's as the unique charm of the Old Woman became known in Buffalo, Rochester, and Syracuse.

One of the earliest fan trips on the O&W on May 15, 1938 is seen here laying down the smoke approaching New Berlin Junction. The train is out of Sidney, and having crossed in quick succession the Susquehanna, and Unadilla Rivers, is now digging in for the climb to the station at Summit. That's still a good nine miles away and our more immediate concern is the junction just ahead, the station barely discernible at the far right. The 29 mile branch from New Berlin Junction to Edmeston will be a concern of the O&W for only two more years. In 1940, the road sold the money losing branch to the shortline Unadilla Valley Railroad, adding 29 miles to their existing 20 miles of track down the valley from Bridgewater to Edmeston. That same year, UV acquired a V class Mogul which they used until 1945 when it was traded in for I class 2-6-0 42, which was kept until 1956. The UV survived the O&W by three years, finally being abandoned in 1960.

Three years later on August 30, 1941, finds northbound Train 9 filled out with local freight and milk as the 313 climbs the 1.35% grade out of Sidney to Summit traversing the mountain which separates the valley of the Unadilla from the Chenango River valley. D.C. Littlejohn's concept of a "railroad athwart the river valleys and at right angles to the mountains" is graphically illustrated by the O&W's rollercoaster profile. The milk train is near the small station of Parker near the top, after which it's back down again for the descent into Norwich.

| NEW YORK 225.14 | **NORWICH** | OSWEGO 99.66 |

Norwich was one of the larger cities served by the O&W. They had competition, initially from the Chenango Canal and later from the DL&W's Binghamton-Utica line. Although Sidney was the division point, the shops were at Norwich. Though they were smaller than the complex at Middletown, they were still quite respectable and had even produced one complete locomotive: a camelback 4-4-0 in 1898. When the first through freight service was introduced in 1927, it called for the O&W to handle trains from Maybrook to Norwich where they would be turned over to the Lackawanna to go west. The arrangement lasted only a short time before the connection was changed to Scranton, a somewhat shorter run. Norwich was the final holdout of steam and on July 21, 1948, the curtain rang down as the 402 rolled in from Sidney and dropped her fire, joining the line of sisters that were moved up to the DL&W connection for their last trip to the scrap

35 SLIDES. COURTESY ROBERT MOHOWSKI

yard. Above, it's twilight once again, for the diesels that replaced the steamers were not the road's salvation. FT 805 is rolling north through the empty Norwich yards towards the freight house and station in the distance. It's March, 1957 and the end is only a few days away.

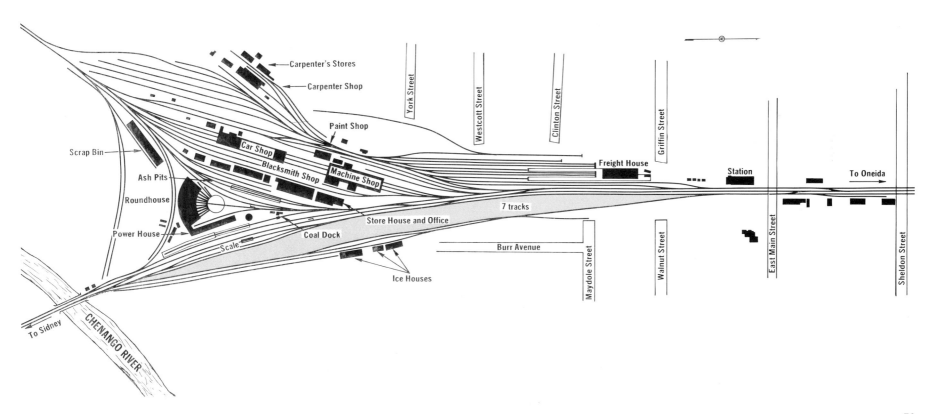

ALL PHOTOS BY JOHN KRAUSE UNLESS OTHERWISE CREDITED

The 323, a W class Consolidation with a Bullmoose tender, poses on the ash pit at Norwich in that final July of 1948. Norwich was the last bastion of steam as the diesels drove them farther and farther north and we can only imagine the frustration of a fan who planned a trip to Middletown or Cadosia, only to be told that the last engine had retreated farther north just the day before.

Northbound Train 9 is stopped in Norwich yard to allow a party of fans from the Buffalo Division of the RRE to inspect the facilities during a fan trip in the early 1940's. Coach 249 bringing up the rear with the RRE's drumhead attached is a Pullman product of 1907, part of an order for 69 coaches split between Pullman and Harlan & Hollingsworth between 1901 and 1910, and the largest single group of passenger equipment on the road. Today it's difficult to imagine that a railroad ever ran here; the area near the engine facilities is occupied by a high school, while to the north, the yard tracks have been displaced by garden apartments. Only the station survives (1976), a storage facility for the nearby textile mill.

D. DIVER COLLECTION, CORNELL U., COURTESY KENNETH L. HOJNACKI

W-2 class 2-8-0 320 in front of the Norwich roundhouse. In the background, sporting Economy valve chests and sheet-metal extra flags, stands a sister 2-8-0 of the neighboring Lackawanna. DL&W's Binghamton-Utica branch passed through Norwich a few blocks up the street from the O&W and in steam days their power was serviced at the O&W roundhouse. The DL&W line survives as part of Conrail (1976).

I-1 class Ten-Wheeler 35 is working up near the freight house as she is recorded on film, perhaps for the last time. The 1904 Cooke product was delivered as a 2-6-0, but was rebuilt as a 4-6-0 in 1919. Note the Ontario Restaurant in the background.

The 311 drifts back south to Norwich with a caboose hop. Just north of this spot, the O&W and the Lackawanna converged and ran side by side for a number of miles. In earlier days, it afforded a grand opportunity for a little unauthorized racing between the DL&W and the O&W engineers. In 1913, as S class Dickson camelback 2-8-0, the 191, succeeded in getting loose from the O&W until its wayward journey was suddenly terminated by a head-on collision with a northbound Lackawanna passenger train. No one was seriously hurt, but there was some mighty tall explaining to be done.

JOHN KRAUSE

Two views of the junction at Randallsville where the Utica branch met the old main line on a wye. When the Midland was originally built, the town of Hamilton refused to bond itself and the railroad, biting its own nose, took the main line over the much stiffer grade through Eaton. In the meantime, local interests constructed a short line from Randallsville through Clinton to Utica, with a second company building from Clinton to Rome. Both lines fell under D&H control and in 1886, the O&W rented them both. In the 1890's it dawned on the company that a simple 3.8 miles of track would connect the branch with the main line again and a wholly-owned subsidiary promptly constructed the Pecksport Loop, enabling through trains to use the easier grades of the

branch. In later years the Pecksport Loop became main line for all but a few local trains. Below left, the date is October 24, 1946 and southbound Train 10 is using the old main as it waits at Randallsville station. The swarm of people on the ground are along for the ride, a fan trip sponsored jointly by the Buffalo, Rochester, and Syracuse chapters of the National Railway Historical Society. To the right, we see southbound 10 again safely in the hole on the Utica branch yard tracks south of the station waiting for a northbound freight. On this trip 10 has come down on the Loop, and the freight may use either the Loop or the old main. The water crane seen at left is directly behind the Sheffield Farms milk cars in this view.

JAMES MCKENNEY PHOTO, COURTESY KENNETH L. HOJNACKI

D. DIVER COLLECTION, CORNELL U., COURTESY KENNETH L. HOJNACKI

Let's take a look at the Utica branch. At the right, FT 807 is north-bound with symbol freight NO-1, the Norwich-Oswego turn crew. About two miles ahead, they will leave the branch at Pecksport and return to the main line again at White's Corners. By this time, both locations weren't much more than a switch and a phone box in the middle of no-where. The checkerboard design on the station is not the railroad's handiwork, but rather that of a local feed dealer who has rented the building. Hamilton was the locale of one of the strangest altercations on the railroad, when southbound ON-2 came rolling through on the night of September 27, 1955 and found the switch to the Leland coal trestle thrown over, just past the station and over the road crossing in the background. An emergency application was futile and FT 803 pounded up the ramp, through the building, and crashed out the rear off the trestle, miraculously landing upright in a field. The crew was only slightly injured and at a subsequent testimonial in their honor, they were presented with EMD-furnished models and a plaque induct-ing them into the "Flying Diesel Corps." The mysterious hand on the switch was never identified and an overturned car from the Nestle plant in Oneida provided plenty of free chocolate for the local young-sters as they watched the clean-up.

The Utica branch terminated near this modest structure next to the New York Central main. The O&W and the Lackawanna both main-tained tracks in this area and in earlier years, the passenger trains of both roads proceeded a little further past the freight house to tie up at the Central's Utica station. The more extensive yards of both roads were out near the city line and were referred to as the Canal Branch yards. Some of this trackage is still in service to reach local industries and the freight house still stands (1976).

It's November, 1945 and a special stands at the Hamilton station load-ing team, coaches, and fans for a trip to Worchester, Massachusetts and the annual Colgate-Holy Cross football game. Utica and Rome scheduled service had been discontinued in 1932, but the O&W ran any number of specials and as late as 1947, new freshman could get within a few miles of the Colgate campus on milk trains 9 and 10, providing the students with an endless source of humor as they poked fun at the curious anachronism that traversed the rural landscape.

Above, southbound Train 10 on the old main at Eaton with another fan trip, this one an April, 1941 excursion by the Railroadians of America. The creamery in the background is another of the large Sheffield Farms operations. The creameries this far north were much less susceptible to the lure of trucking and thus rail service lasted much longer than it did on the Southern Division.

Right: "The Young Girl and the Old Woman." The Northern Division was decidedly more rural and informal than the busier stretch to the south and the enginemen and trainmen had more time to stop and chat, and occasionally hoist a youngster aboard for a ride in the cab. Engineer Fred Rowe of Norwich is seen in front of V-class 2-6-0 284 passing a little time with Bill Wilcox and his cousin Cathy Harrington of Hamilton who've caught their friend at the Munnsville station.

Below, the 225 has just coupled back on her train after making a spot at the Munnsville creamery. The Northern Division was dotted with single-story wooden-frame depots, creameries, and icehouses, very often built by the railroad to encourage business. At many points the railroad owned ice ponds where they would annually harvest fresh ice in the winter for the next summer's season.

Oneida was one of the larger terminals on the Northern Division and the terminus of milk trains 9 and 10. Originally 9 and 10 and counterparts 11 and 12 worked only the Southern Division from the division point at Sidney to Weehawken. Two additional trains, 13 and 14, the Long Milk, worked the full length from Oswego to Weehawken, a grueling 15 hour trip. Sometime around 1930, 13 and 14 disappeared from the tables and 9 and 10 were shoved north to work from Oneida to Weehawken, assuming the old name of the Long Milk, while 11 and 12 also bit the dust, and the dwindling milk business was handled on the head end of 1 and 2 until 1947, when even old 9 and 10, working only Oneida to Sidney, finally ran out of time. Above, the 311 backs a Veteran's Special down to the south end of the yard preparing to return to Middletown on August 18, 1940. Below, I-class 2-6-0 30 (Cooke, 1903) stands at Oneida in happier days with southbound 14. Within a year or so, no. 30 will become a 4-6-0. The station and freight house lay on the north end of the yard just below the overbridge crossing of the New York Central's four track main. After the abandonment, part of the main north of Oneida was taken over by the New York Central to serve some local industry. Oneida should not be confused with Oneida Castle, a station about a mile south of Oneida proper and the site of the O&W's passage under the West Shore and the Utica-Syracuse interurban.

One could see a progressive decline in the size and ornamentation of the stations as the line went further north. Most of the stations on the Southern Division had either been replaced with larger buildings or had been expanded with platform extensions and additions. The buildings on the Northern Division were for the most part original construction and north of Oneida they became even smaller. When the Midland was built, the city of Syracuse refused to bond itself and the promoters went off in a huff and built the line around the east side of Oneida Lake through an area that remains sparsely populated even to this day. The small stations never generated a great deal of carloadings and the railroad dismantled a number of them in the early 1940's. At left, the Sylvan Junction station during a turn of the century rebuilding of the State Barge Canal bridge. The track to the right was the loop to Sylvan Beach, a popular resort on the east shore of Oneida Lake. In the summer, a procession of shuttle trains from Oneida carried vacationers to the beach. The shuttle trains were cut off in 1925, but a Conductor's Special ran to the Beach as late as 1939, and finally the rails were taken up during the War. In the distance just out of sight lay the Fish Creek depot and the crossing of the Lehigh Valley's Camden, N.Y. line, abandoned in 1938. At the right, another typical small station: the Central Square crossing of the O&W and the old Rome Watertown & Ogdensburg line to Syracuse.

Below, "Mighty Midget" 101 is working the east side of Fulton on the relocated main line shortly after delivery in 1941. Originally the O&W's Chicago Limited, nos. 5 and 6, came this far north to a connection with the RW&O at Oswego, but the white stuff we see flying here made a joke of schedules resulting in a service cutback to Earville to catch the West Shore's Chenango branch and later to Utica to catch the Central main. The Ontario then conceeded the folly of trying to compete with six other roads for the Chicago trade in the late 1920's. Fulton was the site of one of the first grade crossing separation projects in the state. Begun in 1926 and completed in late 1928, the new line was relocated to the east side of the city, doing away with 16 street crossings.

At a spot called Nelson's on the south side, the RW&O line from Syracuse joined the O&W; freight was interchanged to the O&W, but the RW&O (and later New York Central) passenger trains had rights over the O&W to reach Oswego. Apparently the Central didn't think much of this stretch, for this stretch was the only place on the Northern Division with automatic block signalling. Although O&W service from Oswego was dropped in 1929, the crews had to watch out for New York Central passenger trains well into the early 1950's. Today, this 12.80 mile segment from Nelson's to Oswego is the longest portion of the O&W still in operation (by Conrail, 1976).

OSWEGO

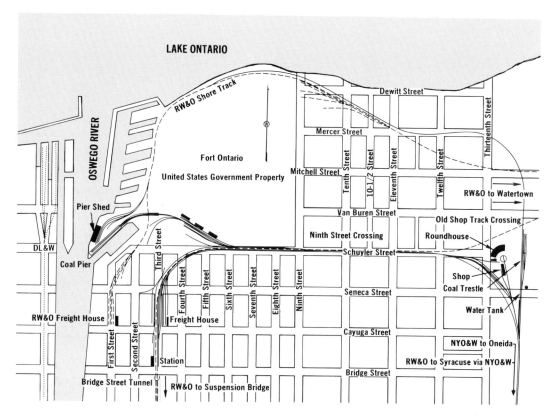

Oswego, the northern terminus of the O&W, was intended by its promoters to become the great port city of the Lakes. It never turned out that way. Canadian traffic had any number of all-rail routings to choose from, and Buffalo became the preferred gateway for much of the rail and water borne traffic from the West, letting Oswego settle for the leftovers. Above right, the literal "end of the line;" our photographer is looking south with his back to the Lake. On the left stands the freight house, and to the right in the distance is the Oswego station. At right, a westbound New York Central plow train stands in front of the station a scant 30 feet from the boundary line where the O&W ends and the former RW&O track begins. The RW&O continued out of Oswego through a tunnel under the domed courthouse past the station and struck out for Suspension Bridge and a connection to four western roads. The O&W shared trackage with the old RW&O in a number of places in the city. It was the *old* Rome Watertown & Ogdensburg indeed, for the road dated back to 1832 and initially connected its namesake cities. In the 1880's they bought at auction a pike called the Lake Ontario Shore, a smart move to get the business from Niagara Falls. Unfortunately they also acquired too much bonded indebtedness and went broke. After passing through a number of hands, the Vanderbilt people started getting worried about who would eventually control it and quietly bought control in 1891. In 1913 it was made an official part of the New York Central.

80

Trustee Lyford in his first reorganization efforts tried to make something of the old dream of Oswego as a great port. The northbound coal business had disappeared long before and in its place, Lyford hoped to capture some of the bulk traffic from Canada and export cargo which could use the improved St. Lawrence navigation system as an alternative to the East Coast ports. During the 1920's and 1930's the state had expended considerable money improving the State Barge Canal and the Oswego waterfront facilities. To take advantage of the situation Lyford's first move was to dismantle the aging coal pier. The O&W owned a large amount of waterfront property and they erected warehouses, docks, and trackage along the Oswego River near the entrance to the Lake. The view above is looking north out to Lake Ontario. The coal docks of the Lackawanna on the west side of the river have also seen better days and will be coming down soon, while on the east side of the Oswego River, the Ontario proudly billboards its new facilities. The Downey Dock in the foreground is a state owned facility served by the O&W while the docks behind it are the O&W's own, occupying the site of the former coal trestle shown in the inset around the turn of the century. The forested land in the distance is the government owned Fort Ontario. At the right, the pig iron in the hold will fill a lot of cars, but unfortunately much of the tonnage passing through Oswego was low rated bulk material such as scrap iron, pig iron, bauxite, and potash which didn't produce much revenue after per-diem and terminal expense.

THE SCRANTON DIVISION

Having covered the main line, it's time to go back and take a closer look at a few lines we passed by on our initial trip over the O&W. Most important was the Scranton Division, leaving the main at Cadosia and heading southwest to the Scranton coal belt. The Division was one of President Fowler's most illustrious accomplishments and was constructed in 1890 by the wholly-owned Ontario Carbondale & Scranton. The flood of coal that rolled off the Division from its opening in 1890 to the lean years of the mid-thirties was the source of much of the O&W's prosperity in those golden years. At the right, a four-unit FT combo leads a northbound freight over the short Cadosia trestle. Coming off the north leg of the wye, it's most likely the Coxton-bound US-2 symbol freight from Utica. While most of the symbol freights were east-west jobs between Maybrook and Coxton, the SU-US trains did a respectable business between the Lehigh Valley at Coxton and the New York Central at Utica, much of it being Canadian traffic. Eight years earlier (February 4, 1940) finds P class Consolidation 220, below, heading for Scranton with a local freight. The two milk cars on the head end are from the far-flung Sheffield Farms operation. Milk was handled as far down the line as Pleasant Mount well into the 1940's. Scranton passenger service was never much and was unceremoniously dropped in the fall of 1930, although the O&W did publish a book similar to "Summer Homes" during the early years of the century promoting the vacation merits of Wayne County in Pennsylvania.

ROBERT F. COLLINS

HAROLD H. CARSTENS

Heading out to Cadosia, there were three miles of track along the New York side of the Delaware River before the Scranton line crossed over to Pennsylvania. Above, US-2 is out of Cadosia for Mayfield and although it's downgrade from Cadosia to the Delaware River bridge, the services of the W class 2-8-0 on the rear will be required as soon as the bridge is crossed. The pusher is on the Sand's Creek trestle just past Hancock station, while the head end is out on the bridge out of sight to the left. To the right, it's the opposite side of the job, SU-1, about ten months later on June 7, 1941 and the 408 is just crossing the state line while the remainder of the train is still strung out into Pennsylvania. The massive Delaware River bridge replaced a longer single track span when the Scranton Division was double tracked in the 1910-1912 period. The 408 has just descended the 14 mile grade from Poyntelle to the river, with retainers turned up to control the speed on the long grade. The bridge lay in a sag and the retainers would be turned down just far enough above the bridge so that the train would be rolling along when they hit the grade up to Cadosia. Bullmouse 352 (below) has stayed on the train from Poyntelle to assist another train back to Mayfield. The Scranton Division was first signalled with banner disc signals. Similar in shape to a Hall banjo signal, a disc in the center of the "banjo" displayed an indication much like a switch target. They also were used on some Northern Division interlockings. In the summer of 1927, they were replaced by three color light signals.

Two miles up the hill and more than ten years later finds the omnipresent SU-1, below, rounding the curve at Lakewood for a meet with BC-3 in the clear behind us. The timetable direction towards Scranton was originally southbound, but around 1927 when the symbol freights were first introduced, it was changed to northbound so that trains heading north from Maybrook and bound for Coxton would continue to be headed in the same timetable direction. The US-SU trains were oddballs, however, and they changed direction at Cadosia, although the odd-number-north, even-number-south designation was retained so as not to confuse connecting roads and shippers. Note that the line is now single-track. The depot survives (1976) as the office of the local justice of the peace.

Above, it's southbound US-2 once again, this time handled by Bull-moose No. 354, who's obviously working hard across the Preston Park trestle in the summer of 1941. The hulking 2-10-2 has less than three years of active life left in her, while P class pusher No. 216, shown below, will survive right up until the final months of steam in 1948.

The hack behind the 216 apparently doesn't have one of those cast-steel underframes, but note that Middletown has applied second-hand passenger car trucks for the high-speed symbol service. US-2 has put eight miles of the grade behind them, but six more miles of 1.60% remain before the summit at Poyntelle is reached.

MAYFIELD

Although trains were received intact from the Lehigh Valley at Coxton and the Lackawanna at Taylor, they generally required some switching at Mayfield and in steam days, a helper or two for the assault on the grade. The worst stretch at 1.33% lay from Mayfield to Forest City, 9 miles of twisting track that followed the Lackawanna River valley. The snaking curvature of the line made it as tough a pull as Red Hill or Young's Gap. The grade eased to 0.80% from Forest City to Poyntelle, and often the "kicker" behind the hack would cut off at Forest City while the road engine and pusher took water before moving out for the 14 miles to the summit. Mayfield was also the marshalling point in earlier days for the mountains of coal that flowed out of the mines, north to Northwest Junction and south to Scranton. A host of mine turns, often running on D&H, CNJ, Lackawanna, Erie, and even Susquehanna trackage would gather up the loads and spot the empties at the maze of shafts and breakers up and down the valley, gathering the loads into trains bound for Utica and Oswego to the north and Cornwall and Weehawken to the south. To the right, a Scranton Division stalwart, P class 2-8-0 no. 208, on the lead at the north end of the yard near the yard office.

A.V. NEUSSER PHOTO: O&WTHS COLLECTION

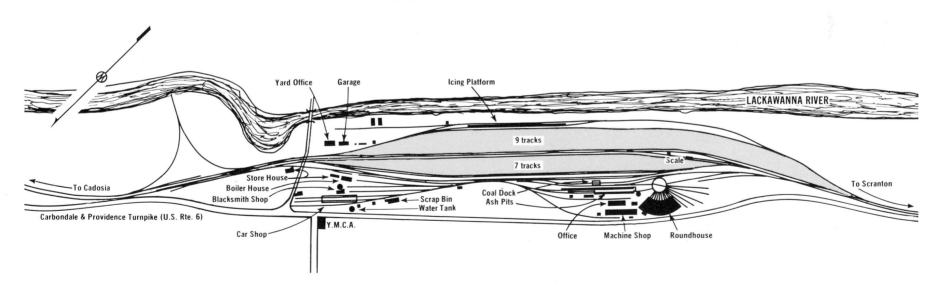

Class P Consolidations were spewing their acrid smoke over the land-scape at Mayfield Yard in the summer of 1941 when this scene was snapped by Stephen D. Maguire, noted railfan and at that time a claims agent for the NYO&W. The large white road initials on the tenders were rapidly disappearing in favor of the white circular O&W herald although the hoppers were showing up simply as "OW." Maguire shot this one from the second floor yard office balcony.

At left, Bullmooses 353 and 358 dig in to get northbound SU-1 under way from Mayfield on a spring day in 1939. The brakeman's lantern hanging on the rear of 353 suggests that the 358 will drop off at Forest City and come back, making the first Bullmoose the one to carry the markers. Actually the drop was made just above Forest City, near the location of the present day Stillwater Dam. Note the back-up headlight recessed into the tender tank and the footboards. The tenders are the larger capacity replacement models that the 2-10-2's acquired in the late 1920's. Below, FT set 808 and a 500 series F3 get a Cadosia-bound freight under way. The date is June 6, 1948 and steam is still working the yard, but will be gone before the month is out. The north end of the yard has remained largely undisturbed in the years since 1957, and has become a small forest as nature has moved in to reclaim her own after the 67 year intrusion of the Ontario company.

As the map below so graphically illustrates, the O&W employed a torturous route to get in and out of Scranton. Their access to the Lehigh Valley and Lackawanna interchanges was almost accidental. The Capouse Branch had been built in 1902 to reach a number of sizeable breakers and was further extended in 1910 from the junction with the DL&W at Cayuga to a connection with the Valley at Austin Junction. When the symbol freights were begun, they employed the coal branches to get in and out of the Scranton area. The trains heading for Coxton were predominantly empties and would use the Capouse and Austin branches, while the Maybrook-bound trains were filled with loads and would use the easier grades of the DL&W to get out, although this routing was by no means rigid. It's something of a wonder that the O&W succeeded as well as it did, employing hastily-built coal branches for hotshot freight service. One veteran engineer reported that a long train on the Capouse branch could be on as many as six up and down grades at the same time! Top right, Mayfield engine terminal in the last years. The coal dock has disappeared but the sandhouse and a portion of the roundhouse remain. Much of the O&W's new steam power from Cooke and Dickson was delivered here for its initial break-in. After the abandonment, much of the property sat undisturbed well into the early 1970's before the march of progress caught up with the deserted yards and empty buildings. Today the entire south end of the yard is occupied by a vocational high school and hardly a trace remains of the once bustling engine terminal. Bottom right, southbound NE-4 has the slack stretched out and is just beginning to move as FT 804 threads her way out of the yard, bound for a date with the New Haven at Maybrook.

GUY P. TWADDELL

GUY P. TWADDELL

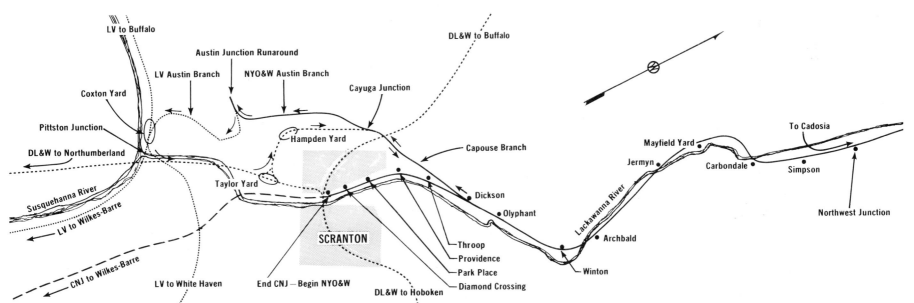

87

PORT JERVIS, MONTICELLO & KINGSTON DISTRICT

ROBERT F. COLLINS

This time we return to the junction at Summitville to take a closer look at the three branches emanating from there. It requires some background to understand the somewhat unconventional operation out of Summitville. The initial problem sprang up when the builders of the Midland decided to by-pass Monticello, apparently deciding that the county seat would have required too much grading and possibly a second tunnel in addition to the expensive and troublesome High View tunnel they were already forced to contend with. Monticello was already a thriving village and to protect their future prosperity, a group of locals decided to ignore the Midland and instead build south to reach the Erie at Port Jervis. The Erie encouraged the project and in June 1868 the Monticello & Port Jervis Railroad was organized. Making good use of the Town Bonding Act that had helped build the Midland, the money was raised, construction was completed and the road formally opened in January 1871. Built to the Erie's six foot gauge, it was operated by the larger road for more than four years, but the receipts were insufficient and aggravated by the Panic of 1873. The road went broke and was sold at auction to the original bondholders in July 1875. The bondholders decided to try again and organized a new company by simply reversing the old name to become the Port Jervis and Monticello. The local folks operated the railroad themselves, changing to standard gauge in February 1881, eight months after the larger Erie converted. Their operation included an 1887 head-on collision whose subsequent lawsuits and equipment damages drove the second company under. It was sold once again at auction and another new company formed, this time the Port Jervis Monticello & New York, whose mentor was none other than Henry R. Low, one of the original promoters of the Midland. Disenchanted with the Erie, and eyeing a number of proposals that would make the road a link in the Pennsylvania to New England coal trade, the new company built a line from Huguenot above Port Jervis to the O&W at Summitville, completed in 1889. Dame Fortune simply refused to smile on the little road and they went into receivership in 1893. It was sold in 1895 and passed through a number of owners, the last ones deciding to extend the pike by gaining rights over the O&W's Ellenville branch and building on in to Kingston. The Delaware & Hudson Canal had been abandoned in 1898 and the title to the canal passed to the Pennsylvania Coal Company which threatened to build a line from Hawley, Pa. to Kingston. The proposed line would have hurt both the Erie and the O&W, so they got together and devised a plan. The Erie bought out the coal company and dropped the idea of a railroad, while the O&W quietly picked up the PJ M&NY and built the line to Kingston themselves. The Kingston branch was completed in late 1902 and in 1905, the assortment of small companies that made up the branches were brought into the O&W fold.

On the opposite page at top, we're at Summitville on March 16, 1941 and a three-car special, one steel and two wood parlor cars, has visited Monticello and Port Jervis on an excursion from Weehawken. To turn the train for the journey south, it was necessary to pull north of the station and back through the wye off the Kingston branch. The train has negotiated the wye and is pulling out on the northbound track to cross over to the southbound main for the trip home. At the bottom, opposite; it's May 12, 1940 and a southbound RRE special from Kingston is dropping down the grade at Phillipsport bound for Summitville a mile or so ahead. The faithful had left Weehawken that morning and gone to Campbell Hall on the O&W, where they got on the New York Central's Walkill Valley branch for a ride to Kingston. Now they're on the O&W again and their train of Central coaches and a diner will cross over the main at Summitville for a hop down to Port Jervis and back before finally turning south to go back to Weehawken: a grand tour by any standards. In earlier years, the engineer of 281 could have thrown stones in the old D&H Canal, for the road was built on the old towpath from the junction as far north as Accord. The 281 was in her last year of O&W service. In December 1940 she would be retired and sold to the shortline Unadilla Valley. The 2-6-0 served the UV until 1945 when they traded the engine back to the O&W for I class Mogul 42.

Kingston at its best and worst: above, U class 2-6-0 no. 255 works the Kingston yard in the summer of 1932. The 255 was one of the few U class engines not rebuilt to a 4-6-0 that managed to survive into the diesel era. The station, freight house, and one stall enginehouse all lie in the distance just right of center. The turntable and water tank are out of sight to the right behind the lumber company in the foreground. The tracks on the left are those of the Ulster & Delaware in the last year of independent operation before absorption by the New York Central. Kingston service had boomed in the 1930's and the company had even reopened the closed Wawarsing station to accommodate the business, but it was only temporary; September 5, 1940 saw the last train pull out of Kingston and the following summer the O&W ran some Sunday specials as far north as Accord before the line became freight-only. At left, the last train over the branch before the scrappers arrived; NW2 120 has brought eight sisters up from Middletown for delivery to the New York Central. The Central purchased all 21 of the NW2's. They survived to wear PC black and thirteen were in turn transferred to Conrail as CR 9263-9275. The bridge in the background was the vantage point from which photographer Eighmey recorded the scene shown above. The engines are standing on the former U&D interchange track. Today the entire area has disappeared under urban renewal. In happier times passengers had a choice of the trolley or hoofing it a half-mile down to the West Shore station to connect with the U&D trains.

89

Beginning at the top left, we go back to Summitville for a look at the Port Jervis and Monticello branches. The junction was quite a place for train-watchers in the first two decades of this century as the mainline trains vied for track space with those of the three branches. In the 1920's the automobile began to make its inroads: Port Jervis trains went out in 1928, Monticello became summer only in 1930 and entirely without service in 1935. The only fares after that were an occasional fan trip and the camp trains to Monticello, a curiosity that lasted into the diesel age. The second photo from left shows a southbound camp train leaving Summitville in the early 1940's, while a second camp special is just pulling in from the branch. The third photo illustrates the ancient truss bridge over the Neversink River just east of Valley Junction station. Built in 1889 by the old Port Jervis Monticello & New York, it was a somewhat unusual design of pin-connected tubular truss members and was in service until 1957, the oldest structure on the line. Just around the curve from the bridge stood the Valley Junction station. Originally the PJ M&NY had built its extension to Summitville from a point on the line just above Huguenot, paralleling the line to Monticello for about four miles on a lower grade until it turned to cross the Neversink and strike out for Summitville. When the Ontario took over in 1903, this proved troublesome as trains would have to go south four miles and turn north to cover the same distance a second time in order to get to Monticello. In 1904, the O&W solved the problem by constructing a cut-off which went directly across and up the mountain on a 3.5% grade to hit the old line at Rose's Point. Valley Junction station was constructed and the old four miles on the mountainside from Rose's Point down to North Huguenot was abandoned. The station shown at the center right is the second station built in 1912. Only eight years was required for the volume of business to outstrip the capacity of the 1904 station. The track to the left leads to Port Jervis, to the right is the cut-off to Monticello. No matter which track a train chose, it would continue to be southbound by the table, and a third track behind the station formed a wye. Despite the proximity of the Neversink, there was no water available at Valley Junction and a thirsty engine had to make it to Mountain Spring tank just below Oakland to get a drink. The photo at right is perhaps one of the best known O&W photos in existence. It depicts the 244 with the March, 1941 R&LHS special stopped at the ice encrusted Mountain Spring tank. Our only regret is that no one on board could record the U-1 Ten-Wheeler getting started again on the stiff grade.

The 244 pauses again at upper left at the Hartwood station. A short distance away stood the home of Stephen Crane, the author of the classic Civil War novel, "The Red Badge of Courage." His brother Edmund was the agent at Hartwood. At upper right, a northbound peddler is just out of Monticello and headed for Valley Junction. It's April 1942, but even the War hasn't done much to improve business on the line. In the final years of O&W operation, a twice weekly job worked both Port and Monticello. At the right, the date is September 1, 1939 and school starts in just a few days. The 246, a U-1 Ten-Wheeler is waiting patiently at the Monticello station for the departure of a Weehawken-bound camp train. The area around Monticello was populated with scores of summer camps, and although summer vacationers would detrain at Fallsburgh, the closest mainline station, the kids were delivered right to Monticello. The freight house in the foreground replaced an earlier structure that burned in 1899, while the station behind it dated to 1895 and was built by the old PJ M&NY to replace a smaller building. Note the single stall enginehouse at left; a turntable and additional yard trackage stood behind our photographer downtrack a short distance.

A.V. NEUSSER PHOTO: O&WTHS COLLECTION

A.V. NEUSSER PHOTO: O&WTHS COLLECTION

Above, U-1 camelback 246 rolling down the valley of the Neversink towards Port Jervis in late March 1939. The Ten-Wheeler and its bare minimum consist look like they might have been lifted out of someone's basement. The single car says something, for Port Jervis was an Erie division point and few shippers could be persuaded to use the O&W's roundabout route. In retrospect, it's surprising that the Ontario kept the branches right up until the end. At the right, the much-photographed R&LHS special of March 1941 at Port Jervis. The train had been turned on the wye after coming down from Monticello and the riders are beginning to scramble aboard before departing for Summitville and home. The track in the foreground continued through the city past the O&W freight house in a southerly direction, then swung in a broad curve to the west to tie in to the Erie. In happier times, O&W trains had rights over the short stretch of Erie track required to reach their station. When the O&W built a new freight house in 1906 to replace the old PJ M&NY structures, they couldn't justify a new station and found it more economical to make arrangements to use the Erie's station. They made a point of seeing that none of their trains would connect with the Erie trains: it wouldn't do to have people going back on the Erie when the Ontario only took an hour and a half more for the same trip.

ODDS AND ENDS

We thought it might be interesting to take a look at the O&W outside the context of normal day to day operations. The next few pages show the Old Woman in a different environment than what we've come to know up until now. At the right, northbound BC-3 is heading west on the Erie past Port Jervis station and pulling by the engine terminal, where the FT is just beginning to intrude on the Erie steam fleet. The date is April 16, 1948 and yesterday morning, southbound NE-6 hit a boulder at Butternut Grove, above Cooks Falls and the New Haven and Lackawanna wreckers are just beginning the clean-up of four locomotives and seventeen cars, so BC-3 (the BC-CB and NE- symbols were late entries in the fast freight business) is going to Scranton on the Erie, most likely via the Wyoming Division line. Below, we're at Simpson, Pennsylvania, just outside of Carbondale. The O&W and D&H were on opposite sides of the Lackawanna River going out of the city and March 19, 1950 finds O&W FT set 805 on the other side of the river. With Challenger 1525 ahead and the hack and E-6a class 2-8-0 no. 1203 behind as a kicker, the trio is attempting to keep a 101 cars of northbound WM-1 moving up the valley. The photo at right shows the Challenger and FT again, assisting train WOX near the summit at Ararat. If they had a kicker out of Carbondale, it probably dropped off at Stillwater, the same spot where the O&W kickers would cut off. This was the point where the O&W and D&H began to diverge, the D&H heading north to Ararat and the O&W drifting east to their summit at Poyntelle. Power-short D&H rented the 807 for about a month to tide them over before the FT returned to its own side of the valley. A soft coal miners strike had left them with plenty of hard coal to move, but precious little fuel to work with.

THREE PHOTOS: ROBERT F. COLLINS

93

Above, the date is May 30, 1942; nine days earlier on the 22nd, a flood had roared down through the Lackawanna River valley and washed out substantial portions of the O&W's Scranton Division. With a war on, the tonnage could not wait for the line to be repaired and the O&W arranged to detour out of Scranton on the Lackawanna to Port Morris, across the Sussex branch to Andover Jct. to follow the Lehigh & Hudson River to Maybrook. The 452 is just out of the reverse curves between Craigville and Farmingdale on the L&HR and headed for Maybrook with 82 cars trailing the Y-2 Mountain. Two days later, the herculean efforts of the O&W men resulted in reopening the Scranton Division, giving lie to the pessimistic predictions of many that the line would have to be abandoned.

Above, it's the northbound Mountaineer, train 3, on August 17, 1946, and the streamstyled days are gone. Train 3 is on the Erie just above Suffern at Ramapo, as the river of the same name flows quietly in the background. Southbound Train 4 is on the ground at Rock Tavern, just south of Campbell Hall, and while the Maybrook symbol freights are not affected, the Weehawken passenger trains have had to find an alternate route. Coming out of Weehawken, a short hop on the Susquehanna brought the O&W trains over to the Erie. At Middletown, they would go back on the O&W again, not exactly the shortest nor easiest way to do it. Train 4, headed by a light 400, went off the rails near Rock Tavern station, and although the locomotives and six coaches were tipped, they did not roll over and there were no serious injuries.

In 1948, the Old Woman played host to the General Motors' streamliner, "The Train of Tomorrow." Introduced at the Chicago Railroad Fair, the train later toured the country. In the fall of 1948, the wave of the future arrived at Scranton and got on the O&W for a trip to Maybrook and then on into New England. Headed by EMD's proven E-7 locomotive and trailing a conventional combination car, the train introduced millions of Americans to Pullman-Standard's new dome cars: a coach, diner, sleeper, and rounded-end observation car. The train is shown at right pausing at the Wickham Avenue station for inspection by the local folk and at far right leaving Middletown for Maybrook. After the tour, the consist was sold to the Union Pacific. A few years later, the competition visited the O&W in the form of American Car & Foundry's "Talgo Train."

Back where it all started: U class 2-6-0 no. 255 leaving Middletown with an eastbound freight on the 14.5-mile Middletown & Unionville. The M&U's relationship with the O&W went back a long way. Originally constructed as the Middletown Unionville & Water Gap, the line served as the connecting link between the Oswego Midland in New York and the New Jersey Midland across the state line. When the O&W was formed, the relationship with the New Jersey Midland was severed and the Ontario got tangled up in the infamous West Shore dealings. Over the years the little railroad got along, becoming the Middletown & Unionville in 1913 and connecting with the Susquehanna at the state line. In 1946, the troubled Susy Q unloaded its interest in the line to a group of local shippers who reorganized the company as the Middletown & New Jersey and promptly bought themselves a diesel, which continues to serve the prosperous little line to this day. The photo above dates January 25, 1941 and in all likelihood, the 255 is on the M&U because no. 6, an ex-O&W 1908 Cooke 4-4-0 purchased secondhand in 1935, is at the O&W shops for periodic boiler work. Whenever no. 6, ex-O&W 24, came home for a spell, the Old & Weary would send one of their lighter engines to the Mean & Useless to tide them over. The two tracks to the right are the O&W mains south out of Middletown, but at the gas works, the 255 will part company with her owner's rails and strike out due south for the state line.

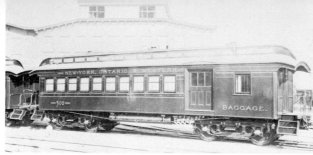

ROBERT F. COLLINS

HAROLD H. CARSTENS

The O&W was well-known among railfans for the Great Timber Fleet, a sarcastic reference to the rival New York Central's Great Steel Fleet. By the late 1930's and 1940's, few 1890 vintage wooden cars could be found running on a Class One railroad. So it seems appropriate that we should wrap up with a brief look at the Old Woman's fleet of wooden relics (and her few steel specimens). To attempt to explain the complicated acquisition and renumbering policy of the road would be a major task, so instead we have tried to give merely a brief description to identify each class.

In the 1890's, the growing Ontario went on a shopping spree to replace the wornout leftovers of the Midland days. Jackson & Sharp of Wilmington, Delaware got the order. Posing at the builder's plant is, top left, baggage-mail car 401 built in 1890. Top center is combination car 302, also J&S 1890. Directly below, car 118, a renumbered 300 series car, performs 49 years later at the New York World's Fair. Top right, 1st 63 (1st and 2nd numbers proliferate the roster) at Wilmington in 1890, while directly below is a brother renumbered to R205 in maintenance of way service in the 1950's at Middletown. Note three windows have been blanked off. The O&W frequented just about every major carbuilder in the process of building up its fleet and in 1892 they went to Ohio Falls. On the bottom row at left, 2nd 58, ex-68, originally a narrow-vestibule coach. The car lasted until 1942 when it was rebuilt as a combine, serving until 1947. At the center, coach 198 ex-1st 64, another Ohio Falls product of 1892, but with wide vestibules. In 1893, the Ontario went back for more narrow-vestibule coaches, represented at bottom right by 2nd 65, ex-75. Like the 1892 order, the few cars of the second order that survived the years were rebuilt into combines in 1942 and 1943; 2nd 65 is still a few years away from the metamorphosis.

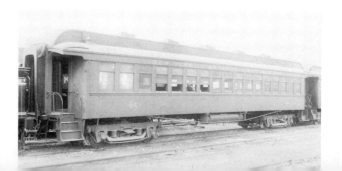

ROBERT F. COLLINS

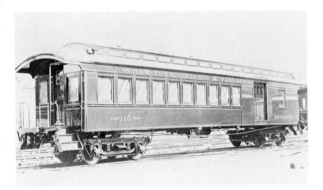

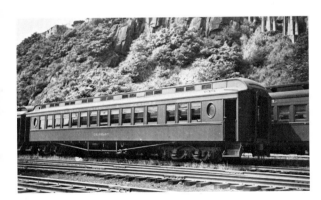

D. DIVER COLLECTION. CORNELL U., COURTESY KENNETH L. HOJNACKI

A. E. OWEN

Beginning at lower left and moving clockwise, vestibule chair car 86 which later became parlor car 86, the "Oriskany," shown directly above the 1897 Ohio Falls builder's portrait. Jackson & Sharp open-end combine 116 was ordered in 1900. At the top of the column, 1900 also saw the arrival of Ohio Falls parlor car 87, the "Oneida," which was rebuilt as a coach in 1942 and sold off to Mexico in 1945, where they were still running when the O&W closed in 1957. The railroad must have liked the "Oneida" for they went to Pullman in 1908 and got a steel-framed duplicate, no. 84, the "Esopus." 1900 must have been a strange year, for the O&W picked up five somewhat different parlors from Ohio Falls, including 2nd 93, the "Willowemoc," shown top left of center. And why is it 2nd 93? Because they had bought five parlors from Ohio Falls in 1898, and after two years rebuilt them as coaches and bought five new replacements. Why they didn't just go out and buy five coaches is a mystery lost to the ages. The O&W next went to Harlan & Hollingsworth, of Wilmington, in 1904 to pick up two more parlors. No. 88, the "Hudson" is shown at top right of center, 88 and 89 filled two slots that had somehow remained blank while the O&W merrily numbered and renumbered itself into complete confusion. The next photo shows combine 120 built by American Car & Foundry in 1902 and 1905 (nos. 120-123). Middletown Shops also got in the act and built two more (124-125) in 1906 and 1907. Apparently, they were good carbuilders for they constructed baggage-mails 158-169 between 1906 and 1909 and baggage-express cars 515-524 in two lots, one in 1912 and one in 1918. The second batch proved to be the O&W's last fling with wood construction. Curiously enough, they had started buying steel coaches four years earlier. Our last photo shows the largest single class of wooden cars on the line; coaches 207-268 were part of a split order from Pullman (207-252, 1901-07) and Harlan and Hollingsworth (253-269, 1908, 1910).

The end: parlor car 83, the "Orange," bringing up the rear of Sunday only Train 37 at Luzon (Hurleyville). Car 82, the "Ulster" and 83 were the only two observation cars the O&W owned, and were built for the St. Louis-Southwestern in 1913. The Cotton Belt sold them to the O&W in 1921. Shown here in the Mountaineer colors, they were later painted to match the diesels and survived through to 1957. The fans seen decorating the platform on a cold February Sunday in 1939 seem to be enjoying their look at the O&W; we hope that you have too.

A.V. NEUSSER PHOTO: O&WTHS COLLECTION

Bibliography
O&W—The Long Life and Slow Death of the New York, Ontario & Western Railway, by William F. Helmer, Howell-North Books, 1959.
Minisink Valley Express (A History of the Port Jervis, Monticello & New York), by Gerald M. Best, El Camino Press, 1956.
To The Mountains by Rail, by Manville B. Wakefield, Wakefair Press, 1970.

Organizations
Those who might wish to pursue the lore of the NYO&W further should investigate membership in the two groups listed here:
Ontario & Western Technical & Historical Society, P.O. Box 405, Franklin Lakes, New Jersey 07417.
Ontario & Western Chapter, National Railway Historical Society, P.O. Box 713, Middletown, New York 10940.